DREAM COTTAGES

DREAM COTTAGES

From Cottage Ornée to
Stockbroker Tudor

◆

Two Hundred Years
of the Cult of the
Vernacular

SUTHERLAND LYALL

Robert Hale Limited
Clerkenwell House
Clerkenwell Green
London EC1R 0HT

British Library Cataloguing in Publication Data

Lyall, Sutherland
   Dream cottages : from cottage ornée to
   stockbroker Tudor : 200 years of the cult
   of the vernacular.
   1. Cottages — England — History
   I. Title
   728.3'7'0942   NA7562

ISBN 0-7090-3286-2

Previous page: Puckaster Cottage on the
Undercliff, Isle of Wight (*see* p.23)

Photoset in Sabon by
Derek Doyle & Associates, Mold, Clwyd.
Printed in Great Britain by
Butler & Tanner Ltd., Frome, Somerset.

Contents

Illustrations

———— ◆ ————

All photographs by the author unless otherwise indicated.

Acknowledgements

———————◆———————

A great number of people have been very helpful in this study: the staffs of County Record Offices and local libraries throughout the southern parts of England; the staffs of the British Museum Reading Room, Department of Prints and Drawings, and Department of Manuscripts, Victoria and Albert Museum Library, University of London Library and University College Library. Special thanks are due to Mr James Palmes and Mr David Dean and the staff of the RIBA Library, Sir John Summerson and Miss Dorothy Stroud of the Soane Museum, Mr John Harris and his staff at the RIBA Drawings Collection and Dr W.O. Hassell who very kindly guided me through the Holkham papers. I have a particular debt of gratitude to Richard Storey of the National Register of Archives and Nicholas Cooper of the National Monuments Register, both of whom have watched this study slowly accumulate and who have both actively contributed in providing guides to new material as it appeared. I have most of all to thank the late Professor Reyner Banham.

Sutherland Lyall

To
Peter

Player's cigarette cards of the 1930s: many, like these, were of cottage scenery. *Top left clockwise:* Steventon, Berkshire; Bignor, Sussex; Weobley, Hereford & Worcester; Steyning, Sussex.

Introduction

——— •◆• ———

A Cottage in the Country

A cottage in the country must be everybody's dream – the idea of a snug little retreat far in distance and time from city grime and city noise, and city routine life: 'a small house in the country, of odd irregular form, with various, harmonious colouring, the effect of weather, time and accident; the whole environed with smiling verdure, having a contented, cheerful, inviting aspect, and door on the latch, ready to receive the gossip neighbour, or weary, exhausted traveller … a porch at entrance; irregular breaks in the direction of the walls, one part higher than another; various roofing of different materials (thatch particularly) boldly projecting; fronts partly built of walls of brick, partly weather boarded, and partly brick-noggin dashed; casement window lights … '

Those are not the words of a poet but of a young architect, James Malton in 1798 in a book called *British Cottage Architecture*. His ambition was to make that dream come true.

Since around 1800, the purpose-built architect-designed cottage in the country in one or another of the Picturesque vernacular styles has been an important feature of domestic architecture. It has been used as a dwelling for the rich, the middle classes and the rural poor. The Picturesque vernacular cottage could be any size from a two-roomed lodge to something approaching a mansion: from John Nash's vast, rambling thatched Royal Lodge at Windsor for the Prince Regent, through the delightful Rose Hill Cottage at Marlow overlooking the Thames designed for a comfortably-off middle-class couple, to the thatched estate workers' villages of Somerleyton in Norfolk and Old Warden in Bedfordshire, and to the two-room peasant-cottage style lodges to be found at the edge of a myriad of country estates in England. Even the first animals at London's Zoological Gardens were housed in shelters which were effectively Picturesque cottages without windows or doors. And council tenants in Britain now find themselves housed in estate cottages of the same style.

Quite apart from size, Picturesque cottages came in a bewildering variety of styles as well. There was the cottage ornée and the Swiss cottage, the Polish, German, Russian and Norwegian cottage. There were primitive rustic cottages, Neo-vernacular cottages and Italian cottages. They came in styles with names such as Gothic, Old English, Plantagenet and Rustic, and there were a few outsider exotics such as Chinese, Hindu and even Egyptian. With the exception of the latter three they all belonged to the same family of Picturesque cottage which in one way or another looked back to the directness, honesty and simplicity of vernacular building as their ultimate inspiration.

'Vernacular' has to be understood fairly loosely, for it could mean the real vernacular of the English countryside or the vernacular of buildings portrayed in the backgrounds and sometimes foregrounds of admired landscape paintings. It could mean the vernacular of other countries. It could be conjured-up visions of traditional medieval buildings – conjured up, for when they were built no reliable evidence existed about their real appearance. On the other hand, it could mean the vernacular of Man's supposed first buildings, constructed from the materials of the Arcadian forest. Or it could be more philosophically 'vernacular' in the sense that the cottage was designed in an innocent, 'direct' and unselfconscious fashion.

The phenomenon of the Picturesque cottage spans the time from the late 1780s, when the landscape gardener Humphry Repton designed such a building for the Earl of Leicester's gardens at Holkham, through the mid nineteenth century, when the great gothicist William Butterfield designed the Yorkshire village of Baldersby St James, through to the homespun domestic design of such Arts and Crafts architects as C.F.A. Voysey and Lutyens. Meantime, in the USA the Stick and Shingle styles developed as a uniquely American version of Arts and Crafts thinking, and there later emerged such individualist designers in the vernacular genre as Bernard Maybeck in Berkley, California, and Ernest Trobridge in the London suburbs. And it is arguable that the Spanish Mission style was an American parallel of the cottagy vernacular style of Britain's inter-war suburban development in the sense that they both sought a source of style in the indigenous architecture of their own localities.

Even now this kind of thinking is visible in the UK, where, despite regular ridicule from the press, many public and private housing designers use Britain's peasant, vernacular architecture as the visual inspiration for new Picturesque housing and villagery. And up and down the seacoasts of Europe, from the Hook of Holland round to Port-Grimaud on the Riviera, developers are still building seaside villages whose deliberately quaint or reproduction houses stand like ghost film sets waiting for the summer hordes

Bailiff's cottage by
P.F. Robinson in
Rural Architecture
(1823). *Below:* A
close parallel (viewed
from the other side)
at Powderham
Castle, Devon.

of affluent seaside peasants-for-a-fortnight. For many contemporary people something like a dream has come true – even if the reality has not the authentic smells of rural life, its drudgery, roughness and too-intimate contact with Nature in the raw.

But for everybody else it remains a dream, the collective cottage-in-the-country dream of the town-dweller. Just below the level of active consciousness it lurks, waiting to be hauled up for inspection in times of reverie, complete with woodman's axe by the porch, cool store by the back door, and the passers-by in the lane outside, the rustic peasants of times of yore. It is the symbol for all that is home and hearth, safety and comfort, simplicity, virtue and serenity.

For those for whom this dream will always be a dream, there is a plethora of proxies, icons, effigies, substitutes, evocations, a myriad of knicknack tokens of its form and symbolic content: miniature hand-carved cottages for the mantelpiece, ceramic cottage teapots, Picturesque cottage transfers for china plates and china *objets vertus*, cottage scenes for chocolate-box lids, mass-produced prints of romantic cottage views in plastic rustic frames. In the 1930s Players, the British tobacco firm, brought out a series of cottage cigarette cards, each with a brief but detailed history of the building they depicted, recalling the immense popularity of the turn-of-the century sentimental painters of cottage scenery, among them Helen Allingham. Today a British building society has used a vast hot-air advertising balloon in the form of a Picturesque cottage, and even the British Design Council, official custodian of good taste, has chosen a cottage tea-cosy for its selection of best British industrial design – the persistent power of the dream quite overpowering everyday judgement about taste and design.

And for full-size cottage-in-the-country builders there was for a time instant thatch. It came in facsimile prefabricated plastic panels.

The indigenous dream

The cottage-in-the-country dream is essentially Anglo-Saxon. The modern European stereotype of the Englishman, learned at nursery school and probably reinforced by the failure of Englishmen to deny it, has as its central image his peculiar obsession with the cottage in the country, along with scones and tea, bowler hats and brollies. The quintessential Englishness was well understood in the nineteenth century: Samuel Brooks, himself a designer of cottages in the country, spelled it out in the introduction to his book *Rural Architecture*. He pointed out that the European who has made his way in life moves to a town where he can make a show with his wealth. Said Brooks with some satisfaction: '... whereas it is the exact reverse with an

Englishman in whose mind the idea of retirement from business and a country life are inseparably united.' At the end of the century Hermann Muthesius was a German commercial attaché whose book about contemporary English houses in the vernacular styles of the time was a sensation in Europe. He made the same point about the uniquely English habit of living in individual houses in the country. It was, he thought, a close approximation to the perfect life – which his countrymen might well copy.

The difference is and was real enough and probably has much to do with the differing social and political structures in Europe and Britain. European power politics have almost always been centralized. In Britain, with its constitutional monarchy and parliament of peers, landowners and gentry, power was long based primarily in the country. Since the sixteenth century the traditional British way of climbing the social ladder was for a successful businessman or merchant to buy a country estate and insinuate his family among the local landowning society which, after a generation or two, was traditionally tolerant about the origins of newish members of its species.

Thus right down the income range the signposts to social success pointed to the country and not the town mansion on a great estate.

New folkways

As a set of broad generalizations, that provides us with a background explanation for the Englishness of the cottage-in-the-country dream, but there were other, more local reasons to be found around the end of the eighteenth century for, although it seems to have its roots in the distant sources of Anglo-Saxon culture, the cottage-in-the-country dream entered British folkways scarcely two centuries ago.

It was inspired by a group of late eighteenth-century Romantic Movement notions about the beauties of 'natural' landscape; Romantic idealizations of cottage folk and their simple life as a representation of the long-gone golden age described by classical writers of the bucolic tradition, such as Longus and Theocritus. It was inspired by Romantic beliefs about Nature as the great teacher of the lessons of life and art. It was also tied up with the new aesthetic notions of the Picturesque which lay behind the greatest phase of English landscape design. And there was the new English landscape painting of Crome and Cotman, Constable and Cozens, and the new Romantic landscape poetry of Wordsworth and Coleridge, Shelley and Keats.

Equally important were the earlier back-to-nature writings of Jean-Jacques Rousseau and his followers. They developed into a strain of social evolutionary theory in the second half of the eighteenth century known as Primitivism. It was paralleled in architecture by a similar back-to-nature theory which, inspired by Rousseau's contemporary the Abbé Laugier, developed into the stripped-back forms of 'purist' Neo-classicism and at the same time provided important visual sources for rustic building design.

At a time of great social unrest in post-agrarian, pre-Industrial Revolution Britain, with the French political revolutionaries across the Channel issuing their Girondiste warcry 'War upon *châteaux*, peace to cottages', the idea of living in a cottage must have had the simple virtue of protective coloration. By living in them, members of the British upper classes could demonstrate their closeness to the peasantry. And by building cottages in a more basic 'vernacular' style for their peasants to live in, they were able to participate in a kind of social engineering: building them inspired gratitude among the peasantry and, providing they were carefully designed to *look* like peasant cottages, had the effect of symbolically locking the peasant into his historic position at the bottom of the social ladder.

At the same time, at the beginning of the nineteenth century, the idea of living in a cottage retreat had a popular parlour vogue. Robert Ferrars, for example, in Jane Austen's *Sense and Sensibility* (1811) exclaims: 'I am exceedingly fond of a cottage. There is always so much comfort, so much elegance about them. And I protest, if I had any money to spare I should buy a little land and build one myself within a short distance of London where I might drive myself down at any time and collect a few friends about me and be happy.'

Architects

On cue in the wings waiting for the Picturesque cottage moment was the young architectural profession. From the last decade of the eighteenth century onwards, in thousands of designs on the ground and on paper and in scores of books, architects fleshed out the cottage dream in a bewildering array of shapes and forms, styles and sizes. They designed them for kings and peasants, great landowners, retiring merchants and small gentry. They designed them for retainers and dependents of the country gentry, as weekend retreats and as the setting for the full-time rural life. They designed with deadly seriousness, with sloppy sentimentality. They were variously chauvinist, fantastic – and often ludicrous. Some designers were filled with concern for the lot of the rural poor, yet others were contemptuous of them. They designed with commercial cynicism and with the utmost aesthetic commitment, with modesty and with flamboyant ostentation. Since then they have continued to do so as the fashionableness of the architecture-of-the-simple-life has waxed and waned.

Design for a cottage (this example more neoclassical than Picturesque) in T.F. Dearne's *Designs* of 1811. *Below*: the real life lodge cottage to Broughton Green Lodge, near Dunton Green, beneath the ivy it is essentially Dearne's design.

The end of the eighteenth century marks several important structural changes in British society. One was the emergency of the middle classes as a significant and clearly identifiable group – and part of that involved the rise of the architectural profession.

There had of course always been architects, but until the end of the eighteenth century it was hardly a calling with either a professional or a corporate identity. Thirty or so years later that had changed completely. By then there was a professional association, there were the beginnings of a formal training system, and architects had begun to prefer people to see them as gentlemen, members of one of the 'polite' professions. And not many years later the newly formed British Institute of Architects was to acquire a royal charter, proof of the profession's new power and respectability in polite society.

At the end of the eighteenth century none of this had yet happened, but young men from the emerging middle classes were beginning to look for careers in the modern sense, and the profession of architecture had started to look like a possible option. What these young architects needed was commissions, and picturesque cottages were at exactly the right scale at which to start.

The other important architectural change was to do with design. In the past architects had designed buildings according to a pattern – in practice an attenuated version of classicism in which changes were rung in the way the detailing was arranged. All of a sudden, at the end of the eighteenth century, architecture became a matter of individual expression: a high valuation was placed on innovation in design, in such things as the style, form and setting of buildings. What better way was there to work out and test out these new freedoms than to design at the cottage scale?

Cottages by the booksful

A favourite method of self-promotion among young architects was to publish a collection of designs for cottages in the new 'natural' style. As many as forty of these cottage books were published between the middle of 1790 and around 1840, when the illustrated architectural magazines such as *The Builder* started publication. They form a charming and immensely informative collection – informative because many of the authors felt it necessary to include a few notes about the philosophic background to their designs, and charming because, unlike the practical eighteenth-century Georgian builders' pattern books, these were for the most part illustrated in a highly pictorial rather than diagrammatic form. Some of the cottage books of the late 1820s and thirties were illustrated by well-known topographical

Rose Hill Cottage, near Maldon, published in Lugar's earlier book *Plans and Views*, (1811). Robert Lugar's Puckaster Cottage on the Undercliff, Isle of Wight pictured in the *frontispiece*, was designed following his clients' attempt to build from the design.

artists, such as J.D. Harding, rather than by the architect-authors, and were often printed in the newly developed technique of chromolithography. Today they are collectors' items and fetch fantastic prices.

They are also of great importance, despite their apparently frivolous subject, in our understanding of that quite profound change in architectural thinking which occurred around the beginning of the nineteenth century: the change from orderly, systematic architecture, which was the inheritance of classicalism, to the architecture of Romanticism. It was an architecture of variety which intended to convey and evoke feeling and mood and express a harmony with Nature.

Cottage books were, of course, primarily elaborate forms of self-advertisement. James Dearne coyly introduces his *Sketches for Public and Private Buildings*: 'About to embark on a profession which of all others must stand in need of the powerful agency of *interest* [patronage] I have adopted the present means of notoriety ... if this book shall be allowed to possess any degree of merit, I entertain but little doubt of meeting a proportionate reward.'

From what little we now know about him, Dearne was to be disappointed, despite the fact that this and several other of his books still appeared on booksellers' lists several decades later. Other authors, however, seem to have found cottage-book publishing a worthwhile venture, among them Robert Lugar, the soon-to-be-successful Essex architect, T.F. Pocock, Francis Goodwin and P.F. Robinson who, in the preface of one of the editions of one

Drawn on Stone by J. D. Harding.

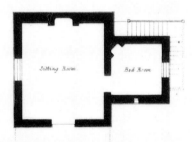

Sitting Room   Bed Room

Two designs from T.F. Hunt's *Architettura Campestre* (1827) and photographs of two cottages in the grounds of Alton Towers, Staffordshire.

of his books, wrote that, 'The more solid advantages arising from my publication have appeared in the number of professional engagements which it has produced.'

For J.B. Papworth, probably the most prolific Regency architect after John Nash, publishing designs soon became a side-line. Writing to his publisher, Rudolph Ackermann, who had run a series of Papworth's cottage designs in his monthly *Repository of Arts, Literature and Fashion* and who was now pressing him to complete a cottage book, he explained, 'It would ruin me if they are made to interfere with my legitimate and professional business. Proceeding with such little works I have no doubt will be useful to myself if not spoiled by too much pressure.' The voice down the ages of the author to his publisher is audible here.

As with many publicity operations, the cottage books had an altruistic front. Their ostensible function was to serve as guides to the new cottage architecture and the new taste. The titles regularly emphasize that they were 'Hints' or 'Sketches' which, in the words of an early author, John Plaw, '... though not one of them should be exactly adopted ... may furnish ideas and may help perfect plans which country gentlemen or others may propose to carry into execution'.

There is good evidence that cottage books were influential not only at this general level but at a specific one as well. The cottages near the entrance to the Staffordshire estate Alton Towers, for example, are clearly taken from T.F. Hunt's *Architettura Campestre*; the gate lodge at the entrance to Devon's Powderham Castle from P.F. Robinson's *Rural Architecture*; the lodge at the entrance of the Kent village of Dunton Green from T.F. Dearne's *Designs*; the Wateringbury, Kent, 'Swiss Cottage' and Elm Cottage near East Cowes on the Isle of Wight from John Plaw's *Sketches* of 1800. Charles Parker's *Villa Rustica* is a probable source for the Chatsworth, Derbyshire, village of Edensor, and the cardboardy gothic lodges to Wivenhoe Park in Essex bear some resemblance to cottage designs by James Malton.

In the third edition of his *Ornamental Villas* (people bought his books as well as his services), Robert Lugar recounts how a couple, the Vines, commissioned him to design them a cottage when they found their builder could not work from the published sketches in one of his earlier books. That was not surprising given the absence of dimensions and the impressionistic rendering of the original design (for Rose Hill Cottage near Maldon). It was just as well, for Lugar designed them Puckaster Cottage at the western end of the Undercliff on the Isle of Wight, perhaps the best and most charming example of the extended Picturesque cottage ever published, in as Romantic and Picturesque a setting as it was possible to find in the English landscape.

Good for self-esteem, though not necessarily good for getting commissions, was the fact that many of the books ended up in the libraries of other architects. John Nash owned cottage books by Malton, Plaw, Gandy and Lugar; John Soane, not a notable cottage-designer, bought a number of cottage books for his vast library, and the flyleaves of many cottage books which still exist bear the names of now-obscure country architects.

The number of Picturesque cottage books still in existence around the country suggests that the well-off public (at £2 to £4 each the books were expensive) bought them and used them as guides in the wave of Picturesque cottage building which was to follow.

Although after around the middle of the nineteenth century architectural magazines displaced cottage books, architects still occasionally published them – though more commonly in the form of books of designs by a selection of architects or in such books as A.J. Downing's *The Architecture of Country Houses* in the USA and John Claudius Loudon's *Encyclopaedia of Cottage Farm and Villa Architecture and Furniture* in Britain. By the beginning of the twentieth century it was more common for cottage designs by a number of architects to be assembled into a book by an editor anxious to illustrate new trends in domestic design, such as Walter Shaw Sparrow's *The Modern Home* published by Hodder & Stoughton in 1905 as part of a series of popular books on art. For twentieth-century architects anxious to bring their talents before public notice, this soon became the standard pattern.

The cottage books and subsequent magazine and book illustrations are important as a concentrated source of knowledge about cottage design, but they represent merely the more immediately visible tip of the whole spectrum of Picturesque cottage design from the drawingboards of British and later American and, here and there, European architects of the nineteenth century and later.

The 'vernacular' tradition

Highly styled to modern eyes though the Picturesque cottage often was, the underlying intention of the designers was to create something which looked like, or at least referred in some way to, indigenous building.

It was an idea which would never have crossed the mind of an eighteenth-century architect or builder. For them, architecture was architecture, and its model was the classical architecture of Greece and Rome, and that was that. In any case there was and is a kind of logical impossibility in the idea of architects *designing* vernacular buildings, because, of course, a vernacular building is one which has been put together by an untutored man using materials which happen to be available locally and in a fashion which follows local traditions – or, as the theorists would have it, by ordinary men addressing themselves to the problem of creating shelter using whatever materials happen to be to hand.

Yet the problems of logical impossibilities were not ones which much worried architects who were designing cottages. Nor later were they much of a worry among influential writers on design. For example, the great Arts and Crafts theorist William Morris in the second half of the nineteenth century wrote, 'It is from necessary, unpretentious buildings that the new style and genuine architecture will spring, rather than from our experiments in conscious design.' And the *Building News* a few decades later agreed, especially at the domestic level: 'The only true way of arriving at cottage designs [is] to adopt the vernacular style, to simply depend on the countryside simplicity and hedgerow ideas.'

In our own century we have had Bernard Rudofsky's *Architecture without Architects*, a study of vernacular building and settlement around the Mediterranean and an immensely influential book for contemporary architecture. Rudofsky extols its qualities: 'Vernacular architecture does not go through fashion cycles. It is nearly immutable, indeed, unimprovable,

Illustration in William Chambers' *Civil Architecture* (1759) outlining the conventional wisdom that the Orders (here the Doric) evolved directly from the structure of the earliest timber buildings.

since it serves its purpose to perfection.' And one line of modern architectural thinking attempts to emulate that immutability by imitating local vernacular forms in one way or another.

And so too back at the end of the eighteenth century. Then the novelty of designing in the vernacular fashion locked in neatly with Britain's newly forming admiration for practically anything which could be associated with the idea of Nature. Said Edmund Bartell in the early years of the 1800s in a passage typical of the thinking of the time: 'If we take nature in a general sense, we may include such objects as by long knowledge become naturalised to the soil upon which they stand ... the baronial castle, the ruined abbey, or the humble cottage, by carrying us back to times past or being combined as objects in a scene become as much a part of nature as the soil itself.' And slightly earlier, in 1798, James Malton, introducing his collection of vernacular cottage designs, *British Cottage Architecture*, the first convincingly vernacular designs ever to be published, diffidently announced that his aim was to '... perpetuate on principle that singular mode of building which was originally the effect of chance' – which is to say, vernacular cottage building.

From the perspective of the late twentieth century, all this sounds like a rather strange and fanciful pot-pourri of ideas and sentiment. And the Picturesque cottage itself is not a topic which can be taken with the utmost seriousness: model for a thousand teapots and toaster covers, inspiration for a horde of sentimental weekend painters and for two centuries of architects and townee seekers after the simple life. Yet it is a central image in one of the great sentimental dreams of modern Anglo-Saxon man and, quite apart from its importance as a means of working out the early detail of one of the most radical changes to occur in architecture, it has been a major source of pleasure for so long to so many people that its vicissitudes are worth charting in more detail.

Almost all these cottage-style experiments with the new aesthetic freedom were carried out under the general guise of 'vernacular' building, but a great deal was made of the detailed differences in style. Architects were anxious to get an edge on their competitors for public notice, and inventing or identifying new variations was a good way of making a reputation.

Over twenty different 'styles' were invented by architects during the first half of the nineteenth century. Some of them were simply fanciful names for the same kind of building. There is not, for example, a clear difference between 'Norwegian', 'Polish', 'Russian' and 'Swiss', or between 'Plantagenet', 'Jacobean' and 'Tudor' – at least not in the new Picturesque cottage architecture of the time. Often landowners built a cottage in one style and described it thereafter as another, more exotic or important-sounding style: a number of biggish rustic cottages in England, for example, are now marked on Ordnance Survey maps as Swiss Cottages despite the fact that they look nothing even vaguely like that original model.

Although the large number of stylistic labels floating around is interesting in that it indicates the new diversity which had come into architecture, there were in fact about half a dozen main styles which can be used as broad indicators of the contemporary lines of interest in cottage styling.

On one hand there was the decorative cottage ornée with curly bargeboards, irregular plan and irregular thatched roof – together with its down-market cousin the primitive rustic labourer's cottage. There were simulated British vernacular cottages, and there were foreign vernaculars – the most popular Italian, the most notable Swiss. And, back on the home front, there developed a slightly more 'architectural' extension of the native vernacular theme in the form of various 'Old English' styles. In addition, from the drawingboards of the less bold, there were a clutch of half-hearted neatened-up styles under the general head 'Modern'. They could wear the dress of any of the styles from Italianate through Greek, Old English and Roman to Modern Gothic but were normally built with stucco plastered walls, newly fashionable in the Regency, which ironed out the pleasant roughnesses of textures and natural colouring of the more authentically 'vernacular' styles, a watered-down, semi-suburban version of the hard-line Picturesque styles.

Of the styles, the rustic, the cottage ornée and English vernacular were popular from the late 1790s. Old English, Italian, Swiss and their variants became popular in the 1820s. These are the rough dates of their flowering – there are individual examples of most of them to be discovered before these dates in surviving drawings. And cottages in one or other of these styles are to be found later, right through the nineteenth and early twentieth century, long after a particular style had ended its popular vogue.

It needs to be said that the Picturesque cottage phenomenon is not an entirely English invention. It is to an extent predated by the rustic farms and villages to be found in pre-Revolution French gardens. These stage sets for pleasurable bucolic fantasies were a common feature in the fashionable *jardins anglais* – English Garden-style landscapes of Europe in the second half of the eighteenth century. There were to be found Swiss farms, keepers' houses in the style of fifteenth-century Germany, Russian houses, Tyrolean mills, Italian vernacular villages and, at Marie Antoinette's Hameau at Versailles, an English village.

These were grown-up, fully developed versions of the rustic grottoes and garden buildings to be found in English Garden landscapes – Britain's first

Primitive cottage in John Plaw's *Sketches* (1800) and (*below*) Elm Cottage at the back entrance to East Cowes Castle, Isle of Wight. Plaw lived across the Solent in Southampton.

serious contribution to the visual arts in Europe. In the translation across the Channel there seems, in some cases at least, to have arisen the misapprehension that the real vernacular shacks and cottages of the English peasantry were part of the designed scene – and should therefore be imitated. When the French garden writer Laborde wrote that rustic villages in French gardens resembled 'those appropriated to the same use which are found in many parks in England', he was of course mistaken, for the English were not to start building real cottages and villages until much later.

In any case, the contemporary and rather proprietorial English view of European rustic structures was: 'too much crowding … more effect than taste'. Working rustic cottages of the same kind were to be built in Britain from around 1790 – and in considerable numbers, but almost as soon as they became popular the Picturesque called for something better, more casual, more natural, less contrived. There was a more authentic model available – the indigenous buildings of the English countryside.

CHAPTER ONE

The Cult of the Picturesque

Today we use the word 'picturesque' in a rather casual, jokey way. That is partly at least to do with its association this century with overly sentimental scenery and painting. But back in the nineteenth century it was a revolutionary theory for landscape and architectural design. It was originally developed as a theory of looking at landscape and then developed into a way of designing new landscapes which looked as though they had come about by the normal operations of Nature over a long period of time. The ultimate ambition of a Picturesque architect or landscape architect was to design in such a way that his viewers were unconscious of the presence of a designing hand or eye. The qualification was that it should be *well* designed. In landscape, Picturesque designers rejected the rockwork and rough timberwork and sham temples and ruins of the late eighteenth-century in the so-called English Gardens – which at the time were noted throughout Europe for their 'naturalism'. As far as the Picturesque was concerned, they were merely gesturing in the right direction. It applied much more rigorous tests of vision.

In architecture the Picturesque likewise almost entirely rejected the classical Georgian past, together with the central classical belief that architecture had its own secret arcana of proportion, language, grammar, and syntax which could operate entirely by and for itself. The Picturesque theorists said that architecture existed in a physical setting and that it could only be designed in the same way as the landscape was designed. It should, said the Picturesque writers, be designed in terms of mass, light and shade, colour and texture – as an integral part of the whole visual ensemble of a new landscape, not as a system of walls, windows and roofs pre-ordained by architectural tradition. That meant that it should be irregular, symmetrical only when that made sense – as perhaps in a street of buildings, that it could be in any style which was appropriate but, following the Nature rule, that it was probably best in the form of a 'natural' traditional rambling English house which looked as though it had been always there. Here of course are to be found the roots of the Gothic Revival as well as those of the cottage in the country.

Humphrey Repton's design for a water-porter's cottage at Holkham, Norfolk, intended to be hidden in a wood adjacent to the lake, its presence indicated only by the curl of smoke ascending from the chimney through the trees.

As the term suggests, Picturesque architecture was designed in the same way as the painter designed and composed a picture. The Picturesque architect's models were not Palladio or Wren or any of the giants of the classical architectural world but the great seventeenth-century landscape painters of Italy and the Low Countries, Poussin, Claude, Ruisdael, Hobbema, Rembrandt. The Picturesque architect's ambition was not to produce a piece of clean-cut pristine building with columns and detailing in the proper places, windows arranged in bays of the right rhythm and the whole perfectly proportioned. His goal was a building of variety, made up of shapes, forms, colours and textures which related to its setting and which took into account the fact that much of the building might be hidden from everyday view by the surrounding planting. At its ideal, a Picturesque building was not necessarily a single form with its own logic but a set of visual components in the landscape scene in precisely the same way as trees, shrubs, rocks and water were components.

Fifty years after the basic principles of the Picturesque had been laid down the perceptive architect and critic Robert Kerr defined the basic characteristics of the Picturesque in his widely read book *The Gentleman's House*: 'The great primary division of all architectural art (and all art whatever) is into the Classical and the Picturesque. The Classical character is that of stately, symmetrical, refined balance and repose with simple elaborated elegance in the ornament. The Picturesque character is that of unsymmetrical, vigorous, sparking piquancy with ornament not so much refined as animated.'

Just over fifty years before Kerr wrote this, no architect in his right mind would have considered designing in anything other than the classical fashion.

Today the differences between Picturesque and Classical are still understood in those rough outline terms, but they are really important only in a design-theory sense among architects, for most of whom both Classical and Picturesque modes of design are freely usable as the occasion demands. Ironically, for the Picturesque versus Classical view, that is what the earliest Picturesque writers argued for when they called for designers to consult the spirit of a place – that is, to develop a feeling for the topography, the history and associations, the colour and contour of a site before embarking on a design.

James Malton's *British Cottage Architecture* of 1798 was the crucial textbook for subsequent cottage-in-the-country designers. The encyclopaedist John Claudius Loudon named him as one of the four fathers of Picturesque architecture, and he was well regarded by copyists in Europe. He was important partly because of the quality and maturity of his designs, partly because he was the first architect to set out the vernacular Picturesque

Design for a small farmer's house in James Malton's *British Cottage Architecture* (1798): non-symmetrical plan, mixed surface materials and a basic plan form which has been repeated by housebuilders ever since.

architectural argument in print, and partly because his brief introduction set out in simple form a gathering together of the threads of contemporary Nature-orientated thought and the new aesthetics of the Picturesque.

Let us look at the major elements of the new Picturesque cottage encapsulated in Malton's text.

First it was designed to blend in and relate to the surrounding scenery: 'to agree and correspond' with it, in Malton's words.

Second it was deliberately designed with an irregular shape and with a casually arranged palette of materials: from brick to dashed and exposed brick nogging (a kind of half timbering using brick instead of plaster), rough plastering and even weatherboarding.

Third it was a form which had become, by custom, 'naturalized' to the indigenous countryside scene – which is to say, it was British through and through: Malton had very deliberately chosen the title of his book, *British Cottage Architecture*.

Fourth it was designed on a combination of the practical and painterly: Malton argued that the exterior should follow the most convenient internal arrangement of rooms and to emphasize changes of direction in the walls rather than make them fit into a uniform façade: '... never to aim at regularity but to let the outward figure conform only to the internal conveniency and rather to overcharge projecting parts ... for on a judicious contrast of light and shade does the picturesque in a great measure depend'.

At the same time, especially when Malton had specifically rejected the whole architectural tradition of his time, there was need for a guiding designer's eye. Here, ready to hand, was the well-understood skill of composition in landscape painting, and for ideas there were the rural buildings and cottages in the admired landscapes of the seventeenth-century Italian and Low Country landscape painters. Throughout the eighteenth century the British had been assiduous collectors of this kind of painting, and any reasonably well-educated person had at least a passing knowledge of it and an ability to discuss it reasonably intelligently.

Normally changes in architecture percolate downwards – for example, the small Georgian house and its decoration are simplified versions of what was to be found in the great neo-Palladian country houses of the time, and they followed on from this new taste which was introduced by the architects of the early eighteenth-century patrons. But in the case of Picturesque architecture, it was quite the reverse. The earliest Picturesque cottages and the theory's architectural extensions, notably Malton's, began to appear at exactly the same time as Picturesque theory was being argued out in public by its chief protagonists.

Personalities

The fine grain of Picturesque theory was laid down during the 1790s and early 1800s in a series of literary squabbles between two country squires, Uvedale Price and Richard Payne Knight, and the landscape gardener Humphry Repton. At the time the poet John Keats likened them to fighting beagles.

In print, at least, neither of the three pretended to have much time for the philosophical positions of the others, and they were at times brilliantly acid in their attacks and counter-attacks, which were aimed at each other quite as much as at the formal ways in which contemporaries designed and viewed their surroundings. In the process the three seem to have had a great deal of literary fun – Repton perhaps less so, for his practice as a landscape designer was under attack.

Yet they agreed on the fundamental points. The differences were to do with detail and with esoteric aspects of contemporary aesthetic and perception theory. Between them they brought out no fewer than thirteen major essays (and a polemical poem) about the Picturesque – in almost as many years. At the time they were widely read in Britain and abroad and they were reprinted on a number of occasions. Today their books remain crucial documents in the history of aesthetics and perception theory.

At the beginning, this set of Picturesque writers and architectural and landscape-design practitioners was a fairly small and closed one: they all knew each other, whether socially or professionally, and often worked together.

Knight, the sharpest of tongue and mind – and most wide-ranging of the three – was a major figure in the circle of Regency dilettanti. Among his other activities in the world of connoisseurship he argued against the acquisition of the Elgin Marbles on the grounds that they were Roman copies. He also left to the British Museum a major collection of antique bronze pots and an equally important collection of erotic literature – the latter to the great embarrassment of the museum managers. In late middle age he built himself a Picturesque cottage on his Downton estate in Herefordshire where much earlier, in the 1770s, he had built a Picturesque gothic castle overlooking a former quarry.

Uvedale Price, a fellow dilettante but of rather gentler literary disposition, was raised to the baronetage in 1822 for political services and lived at Foxley, not far from Knight. He had commissioned John Nash to design him at least one vernacular cottage for the estate and had been one of Nash's earliest clients for an odd little castle with a triangular plan at Aberystwyth in Wales.

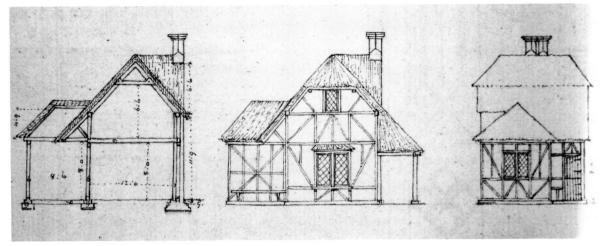

Cottage for Picturesque theorist Uvedale Price in the George Stanley Repton notebook. The fact that Price commissioned this design set a kind of seal of official Picturesque approval on the output of the Nash office.

Repton, son of a genteel Norwich merchant family, had spent some of his school years with the family of the great Dutch connoisseur Zachary Hope. Back in Britain, he turned out to be rather a failure as a businessman: one of his ventures, backing the forerunner of the modern mail service, practically bankrupted him. He was really more interested in living the life of a small country gentleman. But he became an almost overnight success when, in the late 1780s, he realized that he had to earn an income and decided to take up landscape design. He was the first person to describe himself as a landscape gardener.

Both his sons, John Adey and George Stanley, worked in the office of the great Picturesque architect John Nash, and they were probably responsible for many of the smaller Picturesque buildings which bear Nash's signature. Repton himself was a short period in partnership with Nash, he doing the landscaping and Nash the architecture. The two fell out when Nash supplanted Repton as the designer for the Prince Regent's fantastic Royal Pavilion at Brighton, although the sons continued in the Nash office for a number of years.

Antecedents

The Picturesque was not, of course, sprung unexpectedly by Knight, Price and Repton on a totally unsympathetic eighteenth-century world. The word 'Picturesque' itself had been used often during the century – usually with its literal meaning of having to do with pictures and painting, but it acquired a specialist meaning in the hands of the landscape writer William Gilpin. He used it to describe a special kind of beauty – those objects which please 'from some quality capable of being illustrated by painting'.

Gilpin's immensely influential *Picturesque Tours* of various parts of Britain were published in the last decade of the eighteenth century. It was these books which more than any other single influence opened British eyes to the unique beauties of their native countryside. Before Gilpin, the countryside had been merely something which one unavoidably passed through on horseback or coach from one place to another. Nobody thought it particularly remarkable, and even the idea of painting it was slightly bizarre. British landscape painting scarcely existed apart from the hack work of topographical artists, and the one major exception, Richard Wilson, achieved success by contriving to imitate the great seventeenth-century Italian landscape artist Claude Lorraine who, with his contemporaries Nicholas and Gaspard Poussin, had immortalized European scenery. British landscape, it was reckoned, was very small league and scarcely worth the paint.

Gilpin convincingly argued in his *Tours* that, although the Rhine Valley, the Alps or the Italian Campagna were admirable for their sublimity, grandeur or beauty, the British countryside had an equally pleasurable quality of its own: its picturesqueness – that is, a kind of beauty which would look well in a painting. And in his *Tours* he looked at the scenery of his

A P.F. Robinson design for an idealized Old English cottage of two ground-floor rooms and rooms in the attic – and Picturesque planting trailing up the gable and entwining the entrance porch posts – published in *Lodges* (1833).

native country with the analytical eye of a painter and judged views good or bad according to how well they seemed to have been 'composed' by Nature. Most importantly, he pointed out that rather a lot of it was good by these painterly standards – as Constable, Turner and the Norwich School were soon to demonstrate.

An interest in the subject of painterly 'natural' landscape design was not particularly new. In the 1740s William Kent had introduced wiggly paths and rough edges and non-symmetrical layouts into his garden designs and had talked about designing gardens as a set of pictures. Subsequently William Chambers devised the deliberately un-formal English Garden allegedly on the principles of Chinese landscape design and landscape painting. His approach was soon copied all over Europe – the French called it the *jardin chinois* or the *jardin anglo-chinois*, mainly, most Englishmen thought, because of traditional national rivalry. Chambers' near-contemporary Capability Brown, focus of much of the Picturesque writers' detestation, had taken his 'naturalism' further along the anti-decorative path (Chambers' designs were, to modern eyes, rather tinselly) and used in the main tree-planting, earth-mounding, lawn-planting and water rather than architectural features. There were also a number of gifted amateurs such as William Shenstone, Henry Hoare, William Mason and Charles Hamilton who laid out their own informal 'natural' gardens with extraordinary skill and with a clear eye to the way in which they composed as a series of set-piece scenes.

Thus, by the end of the eighteenth century, English amateur and professional landscape designers had given their country a pre-eminence in the design of 'natural' landscape.

Not entirely surprisingly, the Picturesque group rejected almost all of that background. Capability Brown's naturalism, they pointed out, was formula-ridden. It represented simply the substitution of boring stretches of lawn for parterres and terraces, serpentine paths and streams for the old formal waterways with clumps of trees dotted around the mechanically undulating lawn in place of formal copses and avenues. And Chambers' designs were simply ludicrous.

None of what had gone before was sufficiently hard-edged for Knight, Price and Repton. It teetered occasionally, they recognized, on the edge of whole-hearted naturalism. But it had been fearful to take the final step. It had, too, been hamstrung by the prevailing classical mode of architecture. Brown was particularly criticized for his inability to resolve the problem of connecting buildings to his landscape. His tendency was, said the Picturesque writers, to plant lawns right up to the base of the house, burying underground any awkward irregular functional buildings such as kitchens,

Knight: Two landscapes based on the same topography. One paraphrases the bland approach of Capability Brown. The other shows the desirable Picturesque approach where the Brownean clumps have been transformed into a small wood, the Chinese bridge into a rustic structure, the courses of the serpentine river and path to more natural irregular routes – and the smooth mounds into rough ground configurations.

Repton's illustration
of 1816 shows a
simplified irregular
Picturesque
architectural and
landscape ensemble.

service rooms and outhouses – or deliberately concealing them at an inconvenient distance from the house in patches of heavy planting. All this he did in order to leave the 'serious' architectural parts of a house baldly on display.

These utilitarian additions and irregularities in building were the very meat of Picturesque architecture.

In his long and often amusing poem *The Landscape*, Knight illustrated the contrast between the old Capability Brown approach and his own with an early spot-the-difference pair of engravings. They are as different as it is possible for two landscapes to be, yet they are based on exactly the same topography.

The Brownean landscape is made up of an extent of undulating mown lawn spottily scattered with clumps of trees, and with several small Chinese bridges along the unnecessarily serpentine path leading to the house over an equally relentlessly serpentine stream. The distant mansion stands uneasily in the middle of its lawn. Only in the sense that both are rather bald and bare do architecture and landscape have very much to do with each other.

Knight's Picturesque landscape alternative is heavily wooded, the single rough timber bridge crosses a ruggedly edged stream, and the distant attics of the rambling, rather Tudor house peer out from a surrounding wood. It is a landscape ensemble of variety, contrast, ruggedness, of thick planting and open glade, of light and shadow, which is clearly intended to imitate real life: the accidental workings of Nature and Man over many centuries.

Here were collected the essentials of the Picturesque: roughness and irregularity, accident, contrast, a painterly, dynamic balance of light and mass (and, in theory, colour). Here was an approach to design which applauded complexity and variety, which involved arranging disparate and irregular forms together into a satisfying, casual, irregular whole. As Knight neatly put it, '... congruity of parts combined to please the sense and satisfy the mind'.

Irregularity

For architecture the most important external effect of Picturesque theory was what seems on the face of it to be a minor thing – its insistence that buildings need not be formal and symmetrical. Until the end of the eighteenth century that was the only way architects ever designed buildings. There was no question that they could be designed in any other way. The Picturesque writers, not themselves architects, thought that was a ridiculous self-constraint, and said so. Knight wrote: 'That the principal parts [of the façade of a house] should be regular and correspond with each other where all the accompaniments are irregular, and none of them corresponding with each other, seems to me to be the extreme of absurdity and incongruity.'

Knight was in good company in taking this view, for one or two contemporaries had already mused in public about the topic – notably Sir Joshua Reynolds who, in one of his Royal Academy discourses, had suggested that architects might think about the possibility of occasionally designing thus – paying attention to the more felicitous effects of chance and accident and incorporating them into the fundamental design of new buildings.

Unthinkable or not, architects were suddenly presented with an extraordinary new liberty. When they thought about whether architectural 'rules' were God-given or merely convention, there was absolutely no good reason why they could not design buildings any way they wanted. No longer would they have to twist and distort the internal planning of their houses to ensure that the façades were evenly balanced around an imaginary centre line running down the middle of the house. They could plan the arrangement of rooms to suit the convenience of their clients' way of life and could play around with the appearance and form of the exterior in a way which suited and fitted in with the surrounding landscape – or with their fancy.

This iconoclastic view was not shared by all the Picturesque writers' contemporaries. Architect George Saunders, reviewing one of Repton's books in 1804, was outraged. He probably spoke for the greater body of the architectural profession and its clients at the time when he said there was no place for Picturesqueness in architecture. What was needed was, as had always been the case with architecture, time-hallowed Beauty. 'From it results uniformity and order: that is parts supporting and balancing each other and satisfying the spectator or the occupier by an apparent as well as real security.' Furthermore, asked Saunders incredulously, 'Where does Mr Repton begin his much extolled irregularity? For a beginning it must have. Is it a small slip; or is it a corner of the building, taking in several windows of each way? and by what rule does he determine the quality of this regular beginning of his irregular design?' You can hear him frothing at the mouth.

Saunders had not yet got the point that Picturesque design was not about starting from a point on a piece of drawing paper or a level or a central line: it was about the whole appearance of a building as a three-dimensional thing. The 'beginning' for Picturesque design was of a different order: the local scene, convenient planning, the lesson of vernacular or medieval builders, the shape of local planting, not the geometry of the drafting board. And it was about the relationship between the architecture and the landscape.

On the other hand, Saunders had a point. Abandoning the formulas and rules of traditional architecture invoked the spectre of unbridled architectural licence. Some of the more amusing cottage designs demonstrate that there was nothing particularly wrong with that. But the Picturesque writers had anyway anticipated the point. Knight, a little worried about what he and his Picturesque compatriates had started, reminded architects that the Picturesque was not about the complete abandonment of constraints in design. There were the lessons and disciplines of painting as a guide. Indeed, Price had called for the training of a new kind of architectural being: the *architetto-pittore*, the architect who was also a trained painter, who understood the rules of painterly composition and balance as well as good building.

Since the Baroque, painters had understood the way in which they could compose their scenes in a way which 'balanced' by using colour, shape, form, intensity, light and shade – not by starting off at the middle and making all the things on one side balance those on the other. It is a process called dynamic balance, and it was particularly well understood in eighteenth-century Britain because of the popularity of seventeenth-century landscape painting which deployed dynamic balance as a matter of course. Although painters and *cognoscenti* of painting understood it and its mixture of simple rules and intuition, architects had ignored its possibilities. Yet here was the solution to both the problem of Saunders' 'starting point' and the problem of unrestrained freedom.

Knight argued that this '… affords so wide a field for the licencious deviations of whim and caprice, it may be discreet always to pay some attention to authority – especially where we have such authorities as those of the great landscape painters … the study of whose works may at once enrich and restrain invention'. He was giving a fairly broad hint that architects might look not only at the techniques of composition but at the buildings to be found in these paintings. They might well serve as models for real buildings.

Here was a crucial set of ideas based on a fresh, sideways look at the problem of taste, vision and perception. The vernacular cottage had been transformed from its undistinguished, unavoidably everyday role into the realms of high art. And in that process the face not only of cottage design but of the whole of architecture was to be changed.

Primitivism

The Picturesque's interest in nature, vernacular and directness was influenced by the social theories of Jean-Jacques Rousseau published in the second half of the eighteenth century. Rousseau argued that it was only by returning to the simplicity of Original Man's ingenuous state that modern society could be reformed, that Nature was the great teacher and that by communicating with Nature modern man could come to a better understanding of himself and his future.

In practice Rousseau's was not a name to bandy around in Britain at the time because it was so closely allied with the philosophy of the French Revolution. But that of one of his disciples, the Swiss melancholic Johann Georg Zimmermann, was acceptable: translations of his book *On Solitude* (*Über die Einsamkeit*) ran to a score of editions in early nineteenth-century Britain. It was popular because his name was not Rousseau and because his message lacked Rousseau's hard line – and seemed therefore to be practical. Now almost completely unknown and about as unreadable as any eighteenth- or nineteenth-century book of sermons, it was little more than a watering down of the basic Rousseauesque message about how innocent man had been corrupted rather than advanced by his progress from the primitive state. Zimmermann pitched his message at a more workaday level. For him, man was trivialized by modern life and its fashions and manners. The answer was to retire from the world (even if only for a short period of time), to a rural solitude, to a cottage in the country: 'Left to reflect in the calmness and sobriety, during the solitary hour, upon the false joys of deceitful pleasures ... he would soon perceive and candidly acknowledge their nothingness and insipidity; he would soon behold the pleasures of the world in their true colours.... In the rural retreat [for where else should all this take place?], the shepherd and the king should live on equal terms.'

Zimmermann set the seal on his literary popularity by retiring from the world for good by committing suicide in 1795 – the ultimate Romantic act.

Contemporary Romantic literature and poetry were, of course, full of that kind of thing, and Zimmermann's importance was less as an original thinker than as a widely popular preacher of the Rousseauesque back-to-nature doctrine in a form palatable to middle- and upper-class people – the potential builders of rural retreats.

Designing convincing vernacular cottages really required an architect, ideally someone who was trained in the basics of painterly composition and who had a well-developed three-dimensional sense as well as the standard knowledge of building construction. He would base his design loosely on an amalgam of idealizations of real vernacular or traditional buildings tempered

The frontispiece to
the original 1755
French edition of
Laugier's *Essai:*. A
personification of
Nature directs the
reader's attention to
the first example of
architecture – less
systematic than the
English illustration –
and presumably
approved by Laugier

by what he knew of the shape and form of cottages to be found in approved old landscape painting, the nature of the surroundings plus his own intuition and the possible interesting external shapes which the plan of his accommodation might produce.

But for lazier or simpler souls there was also another visual source to be plundered. It was in a sense the original vernacular – the primitive hut of Original Man. Nobody, naturally, had any idea what this might have looked like, but practically all educated Englishmen in the late eighteenth century believed that they had a good idea of what it was supposed to have looked like. For there was a long literary tradition that it was the timber precursor of the Greek Doric temple, and illustrations of it were to be found in the many translations of the *Ten Books on Architecture* by Vitruvius (the classical Roman writer on architecture) and in a group of serious architectural books of the time.

Joan Soane's design for a dairy at Betchworth Castle. Similar in spirit to his Hamels dairy, it clearly demonstrates the connection between Man's first direct essay at architecture and the basic elements of the Greek temple.

As the eighteenth century liked to believe it, this first of all buildings was a simple little structure with a gable roof of branches and leaves, stout upright tree trunks at the four corners and a rough infilling between them forming walls. It was not that people believed that this was precisely what the first man in the Arcadian forest built for himself, but that this was a convenient image to hold in mind – especially when it clearly showed that the classical tradition in architecture, based as it was on the architecture of Greece and later Rome, sprang ultimately from Nature.

Symbols and realities are readily mixed up, and where better than in English Gardens of the mid-eighteenth century which were beginning to veer in the direction of naturalism? Anybody who had been around up-to-the-minute English Gardens of the time would almost certainly have come across little 'hermitages' in the form of the rustic primitive hut – imitations carefully constructed from roots and branches and positioned at the ends of vistas or at the entrance to groves. Their purpose was less practical than symbolic, for they acted as signposts in 'naturalistic' gardens, reinforcing the idea of the presence or guiding hand of Nature.

It needs to be said that Picturesque commentators of the early nineteenth century were contemptuous of both this kind of crude symbolism and the artificiality of the root-and-branch simulacrums. On the other hand the symbolism of the primitive hut was so well understood that it was difficult for the following architects to give it up entirely, and vestiges and even quite substantial elements of it – for example, the rough tree-trunk corner supports and the thatched roof – were to be found in the simplest kind of Picturesque cottage well into the nineteenth century.

The more-than-passing resemblance of this little hut to the simple Doric temple is an important side issue, for the story of the building of the first hut by Original Man was turned into a parable by the French architectural writer the Abbé Laugier. Laugier was a contemporary of Jean-Jacques Rousseau, and his mid-century *Essay on Architecture*, widely read throughout Europe and translated into English in the same decade, followed the same lines as Rousseau's *Essay on the Arts and Sciences*. It argued that architecture had to return to its fundamental roots in Nature in order to become significant once again. In the essay Laugier turned Vitruvius's generalizations about the probable origins of architecture into a specific story.

He sets the scene with First Man sprawled on the lawn enjoying the simple pleasures of the grass, the sun and the gentle wind. These delights are not to last, for Laugier's Man begins to discover that the sun has started to burn him. He retreats to the shade of a nearby leafy bush and is once again at one with Nature. But suddenly a rainstorm blows up. Disconcerted, he dives into a nearby cave for shelter. Waiting for the storm to pass, he suffers the first

Frontispiece to the English edition of Laugier's *Essay on Architecture*. The basic form of the Greek Doric temple is (deliberately) unmistakable.

bout of claustrophobia in this close atmosphere and eventually emerges into the now clear and dry air having learned several things. The most important is that, for Nature to be wholly beneficent, she needs a little help. And so he starts on the construction of the first building – a little structure which will shelter him from the sun and the rain and yet avoid the oppressive air of the overhanging cave. The little hut with its roughly thatched roof and four supporting tree trunks at the corners is the first essay in architecture.

Thundered Laugier: 'The little rustic cabin I have just described is the model upon which all the magnificences of architecture have been imagined. It is by coming near in the simplicity of this first model that we lay hold on true perfection.'

Subsequently major architects and designers such as Ledoux and Schinkel and, in Britain, John Soane, were to follow this argument to one of its logical theoretical conclusions in the form of purist Neo-classicism – the ultra-severe architecture (paralleled in painting and sculpture) of the early nineteenth century, which relied on massively simplified detailing and forms, a rejection of the more decorative elements which had been introduced to the classical tradition over the preceding three centuries, and a plainness of form intended to create a powerful impact on the viewer's mind as much as his vision.

On the other hand, in other hands and at a more simplistic level, Laugier's parable could be translated literally into an argument for building in a 'primitive' vernacular style – which was not his intention at all. He was arguing about high architecture returning to the simplicity and spartan quality of its classic models. The hut story was a parable, not an incitement for people to build decorative imitations of it. Had he lived into the nineteenth century, Laugier would almost certainly have been horrified that his writing could have been understood to reinforce in a general way the virtues of building Picturesque cottages, for the Picturesque represented the antithesis of his severe, spartan, classic architectural philosophy.

Whatever Laugier might have felt, the sophisticated mind of the later eighteenth century was tickled by Rousseau's idea that it had got it all wrong and that it could be taught great truths by getting back to basics. The discoveries of explorers in the New World seemed to confirm this general thesis, for in the New World were to be found contemporary versions of Original Man in the form of unsophisticated races who rapidly became, in European eyes, the species Noble Savage. And their habitations, built from the materials of the locality – palm branches here, turf there and blocks of ice there – provided a kind of generalized proof of the Primitivitist architectural argument, just as their social behaviour proved Rousseau's point.

It was not long before European peasants – the Swiss, Russians, Poles, Norwegians, Corsicans and even Scots – began to acquire a kind of honorary Noble Savage status as well, which was to focus attention on their traditional buildings as exemplars of natural architecture.

———— ✦ ————

CHAPTER TWO

Art Imitating Nature: The Vernacular Cottage and the Rustic Cottage

For most people there is nothing very special about vernacular building. It is the way ordinary local builders built ordinary buildings from the locally available materials: stone in the Cotswolds, thatch in Norfolk, timber in Essex, adobe in California and so on. It is unsophisticated and regional so that, strictly speaking, in the western world vernacular building came to an end around the middle of the nineteenth century when the canals and railways made it possible to transport building materials cheaply all over the country.

Before that, ordinary country people could build no other way. Usually they built their cottages themselves – especially if they were settlers and squatters – and what they did build was so ramshackle that it scarcely qualified as building. There was no national consistency about vernacular building: it varied widely in appearance from one place to another according to what basic building material happened to be locally available. And, because even the most elaborate version of it followed slow-moving craft traditions, it was never thought of by the educated as having anything remotely to do with architecture or as having the slightest importance.

Not, that is, until the very end of the eighteenth century. Then the Picturesque writers began to notice that vernacular buildings were a regular feature of admirable real 'natural' landscapes – and an important subject in their favourite seventeenth-century landscape paintings. Around the same time Constable and the Norwich School, the new indigenous school of landscape painting, were painting vernacular cottages as a matter of course, and Royal Academy annual exhibition catalogues of around the turn of the century show that cottages and cottage subjects were of increasing interest for English artists in general.

The Picturesque writers also recognized that vernacular building came about in a way which was closely analogous to Nature's way of operating. It was a direct, almost instinctive way of going about things. Vernacular buildings merged in so very naturally with real landscape surroundings because over the years Nature herself gave a helping hand: creepers and lichens grew, and the materials making up the walls, roofs, windows and doors were eroded by the elements. Gently battered by wind, rain, snow and

A Malton design for a two-room labourer's cottage intended to be located in a wood, constructed and surfaced in a miscellany of 'natural' materials.

sunshine, they grew mellow and stained – and, when they were unoccupied for any time, began to decay back into the mother earth from which they had been created. Vernacular buildings 'grew' in the same way as plants and trees grew – in the hands of succeeding occupants, who, over the years, added *ad hoc* alterations and additions here and there as they became necessary.

Thus vernacular building had significance for anybody who believed that moral virtues were to be found in the idea of Nature and that moral lessons were to be learned from Nature and amid Nature. For anybody who was not quite sure what might follow from all this, a group of Picturesque architects had the answer. It was to build new cottages in the 'vernacular' style.

The landscape gardener Humphry Repton and his then partner John Nash had been designing and occasionally building Picturesque vernacular cottages for clients during the 1790s. But it was James Malton who published the first serious sets of designs in 1798 in his book *British Cottage Architecture*. 'I am most forcibly influenced', he said, 'by a desire to perpetuate the peculiar beauty of the British, Picturesque, rustic habitations, regarding them, with the country church, as the most pleasing, the most suitable ornaments of art that can be introduced to embellish rural nature.'

Not entirely surprisingly, the book was reviewed with something akin to horror by most architectural commentators. Just one reviewer, clearly sympathetic to the Picturesque, had a nose for the future direction of domestic architecture. He wrote about the need to '... propagate true taste ... let a style of architecture as particularly adapted to rural scenes be inculcated, and the doctrine will spread and at last become fashionable ... ', as indeed it did.

James Malton's designs for four peasant cottages based on the same plan and form. They show what visual variety could be achieved with a simple irregular plan and the arrangement of a selection of different vernacular materials.

Malton's designs ranged in size from two-room cottages to a thatched two-storey house for a 'large and opulent family', which, he claimed, united elegance of form with 'cottage construction and simplicity'. He was naturally enough keeping his potential client options open, and he included several straightforward symmetrical houses on the grounds that some people liked that kind of thing. They were not, he said 'entirely to my own mind'.

Coupled with the irregularity of shape was a deliberate casualness in the type and combination of materials which made up the exterior: brick nogging (a kind of half timbering with brick infill panels), weatherboarding, stucco (carefully streaked to simulate age), thatch, slate, tiling and brick. Unlike all designed houses until that time, Malton used them in combination with each other – brick for one projecting section of the façade wall, streaked stucco for the rest, weatherboarded lean-tos, slate for a main roof, thatch for a side room. And in his first group of designs for peasants' huts, all based on the same plan, he showed how easy it was to create quite different visual effects simply by rearranging the selection and combinations of walling and roofing materials.

Malton was none too worried if clients decided to go for alternative surface treatments – or even for variations on the plan. Octagonal bows could be happily substituted by circular or square bows. In the best vernacular tradition change and variation were quite proper, '... till from knowledge of conveniences wanted and ideas here furnished, a handsome dwelling may be constructed ... though not at all resembling any one design given here.' Even the formal, symmetrical designs could be rendered picturesquely irregular by leaving off a room on one side.

Here were designs quite unlike any others before published – or for that matter many others built. They were, indeed, as Malton had promised in his introduction, 'an attempt to perpetuate on principle, that peculiar mode of building which was originally the effect of chance'.

In terms of technical composition they were also highly accomplished designs. That was understandable, for Malton's track record was rather more in topographical illustration than architectural practice. Brought up in Ireland, he came of a family of topographical artists. Both his father and his brother were well known, brother Thomas for his illustrations of London and the fact that he taught the principles of perspective to the artists Turner and Girton at his school in St Martin's Lane.

As many artists in the half-century before him had done, Malton had tramped around Britain making topographical sketches. He had also brought out a rather potboiler instruction manual on perspective and drawing in 1800 called *The Young Painter's Mahlstick*, two years before his second and rather bizarre book *Designs for Villas*. He exhibited at Royal

Academy shows from 1792, the year he came to London from Ireland, until his suicide in 1803. From 1798 onwards the subjects of his exhibits at the RA were all designs for cottages.

With this background in painting and illustrating as well as architecture, here was something approaching the *architetto-pittore* – the designer whom Price had envisaged as the ideal picturesque architect, trained in the skills of painterly composition as well as architecture. Sadly Malton seems never to have been very successful at either, although the later great encyclopaedist John Claudius Loudon was to set him beside Knight and Price and Repton as a founding father of Picturesque theory.

Malton's *British Cottage Architecture* was the first and most outstanding of vernacular cottage-book designs. But there were others around the beginning of the nineteenth century: Edmund Bartell's *Hints for Picturesque Improvements in Ornamented Cottages* of 1804 and William Allanson's *Views of Picturesque Cottages with Plans* of 1805. Bartell's book was really a set of essays on the Picturesque and on cottage building with a few illustrations – of cottages in the rustic rather than vernacular fashion. Atkinson's rather odd little book contained a few offhand plans for what appear to be sketches of real vernacular cottages.

A design for a vernacular cottage in William Atkinson's *Views of Picturesque Cottages* (1805) with modest Gothic details based, he claimed, on drawings he had done of scenery around the country.

For any architect who wanted source material for vernacular cottage design there were the engravings of James 'Antiquity' Smith, the first set of which came out in 1797, the year before Malton's book, and which Malton mentions approvingly. This set was published with a brief text under the title *Remarks on Rural Scenery* and contained etchings of tumbledown cottages to be found around the outskirts of London. Smith says that they were all taken from Nature and were etched on the spot. He was to continue publishing this kind of set for two decades, both cottages and cottage scenery and the 1815 set *Etchings of Remarkable Beggars*.

Viewed objectively, what Smith made his money from was portraying grinding poverty and its meagre accessories. He was slightly uneasy about that and rather carefully pointed out that the artist was concerned only with the visual qualities of what he painted: '... patched plaster ... various tints and discolorations ... weatherbeaten thatch ... The unrepaired accidents of wind and rain offer far greater allurements to the painter's eye.'

Other artists, such as Francis Stevens, Robert Hill, John Varley, Paul Sanby Munn, W.H. Pyne and Samuel Prout, soon followed suit and by the 1820s were beginning to suggest, not unreasonably, that they were doing for fine art what the contemporary stream of Nature poets and writers were doing for landscape literature. What had happened was that – in their hands

A vernacular cottage from Edmund Bartell's *Hints for Picturesque Improvements* (1804).

and in those of Constable and the Norwich School and, in a slightly different way, Turner – they had turned topographical illustration from a low-grade hack trade into a respectable form of art. And so too architects had transformed the humble cottage into a model for a serious branch of architecture.

Their precedents were the paintings of the Low Country painters of the seventeenth century: Hobbema, Ostade, Wouwermanns and Rembrandt rather than the slightly grander Italians, Claude Lorraine and the Poussins. These were the sources used by Malton and many Picturesque architects who sought to show that their work had a long and serious visual tradition of its own quite apart from its intrinsic merits as an aspect of Nature.

Vernacular cottages also appeared in cottage books by Pocock and Lugar and among the later Old English designs by Robinson, Hunt and Goodwin. It is not a particularly easy style to define in these books for, following the conventional rules of social caste, the Old English style (or, in the case of the earlier books, the cottage ornée style) was for the gentry, vernacular a down-market version for peasants. As was the case with all the Picturesque styles, this hierarchical rule was not followed rigidly. When, for example, the vast and rambling Royal Lodge at Windsor, designed by John Nash for the Prince Regent, was pulled down, it was replaced by a commodious cottage in a distinctly vernacular style.

For Malton, who was breaking entirely new ground in even suggesting that vernacular building should serve as a model for new building, the vernacular had a great deal of mileage, but for subsequent cottage book architects, anxious to demonstrate their versatility, the more elaborate and architecturalized styles naturally won more attention.

Although Malton was the first designer to devote a book to the topic of vernacular design, Humphry Repton, the great designer of Picturesque natural landscapes, had worked it all out already. In 1789 he had designed the first (as far as we know, first ever) vernacular cottage, as part of his proposals for the landscape at Holkham Hall which he prepared for the Earl of Leicester. It was his second serious commission as a landscape designer but this part of his scheme seems never to have been built.

The Holkham cottage was intended as the home of a water porter and his family in a clearing in the wood bordering the great lake. The porter's job was to be to look after the nets and the pleasure boats – 'a sort of Aquatic gamekeeper', wrote Repton. The cottage, he said, '… should be so picturesque embosomed among the trees that it shall be totally invisible from the house [the William Kent-designed Holkham Hall] and from the lake itself; yet from these points the occasional column of smoke which ascends from the chimney will be a charming moving object'.

A vernacular double cottage by W.F. Pocock published in his *Architectural Designs* (1807). The front façade is mirrored on the back.

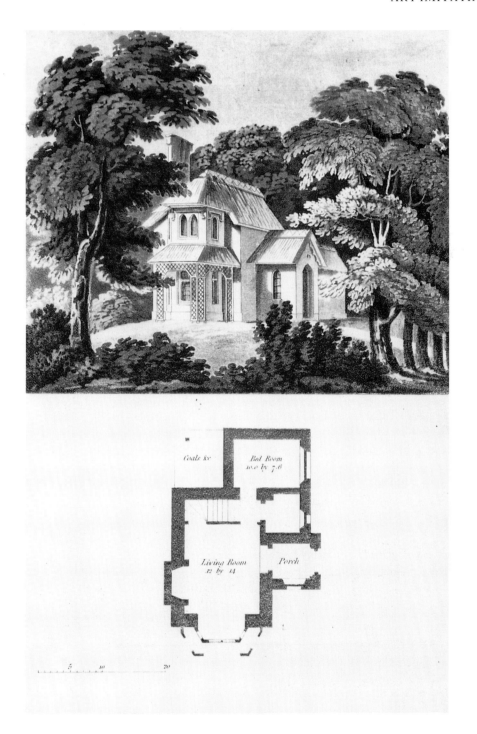

Picturesque cottage by Robert Lugar published in *Plans and Views* (1811). This cottage has two ground-floor rooms – one of the virtues of irregular Picturesque design was that it gave small dwellings the appearance of being larger.

Humphrey Repton's design for a woodman's cottage at Blaise Castle, built *c.*1797 nestling at the edge of a wood, smoke rising through the trees, its simplicity the effect of apparent rather than real neglect and accident.

Having set the scene and emphasized that the cottage was an object in the landscape – whose presence was suggested rather than plainly seen, Repton went on to describe this first of vernacular cottages with its sunken and eyebrowed thatch roof, irregular walls in brick nogging, windows and doors peeping out from the thick overcoat of climbing plants: 'It will appear', proclaimed Repton, 'the habitation of Industry, with an affectation, rather than the reality of Penury.' In order that visitors should not mistake it for the real Norfolk vernacular, he was at pains to point out that its appearance was based on fishermen's huts he had seen in the West Country, not in the locality.

Never built, the Holkham cottage was nevertheless illustrated in Repton's widely read *Fragments and Hints on Landscape Gardening* published in 1794, and it must have been a major inspiration for James Malton, who was a keen student of all the contemporary Picturesque writing.

There was another quite sensible reason for building vernacular cottages in new landscapes. It was to give these landscapes the life and movement which real natural landscapes always have. Repton was laughed at by his critics for bothering to discuss the visual importance of animals as moving objects in his landscapes, but his point was an important one for landscape which was designed to look as though it had been nature's work. So too, he thought, was the presence of people, and for this circumstance he coined the rather awkward word 'inhabitancy'. He outlined this point in putting his case for building a woodman's cottage in the landscape at Blaise Castle, near Bristol. It was actually built, probably in 1797. Writing afterwards he said, 'Some object was needed to enliven the scenery. A temple or a pavilion in this situation would have reflected the light and formed a contrast with the dark woods. But such a building would not have appeared to be inhabited. This cottage therefore derives its chief beauties from that which cannot easily be expressed by painting – the idea of motion, animation and inhabitancy.'

'Its form', he went on carefully, 'is meant to be humble without meanness. It is and appears to be the habitation of a labourer who has care of the neighbouring woods. Its simplicity is the effect of art – not of neglect or accident.'

Repton should perhaps have added that it was art imitating neglect and accident – the affectation of penury without the reality. In fairness to the Repton and the Picturesque writers it should be said that, whenever it was possible, they expressed a concern that their Picturesque improvements should not displace the peasantry – and that Picturesque building should be aimed at improving their physical lot.

It is not altogether easy to identify good examples of Picturesque vernacular cottages today. The best examples are presumbly now indistinguishable from the real thing because they have been altered or added to, thatch replaced with tiles or slate, verandas filled in, timberwork replaced with other details or materials. There is also the problem that what was a credible facsimile of a vernacular cottage to early nineteenth-century eyes would probably look rather artificial today. But we do know that Repton's one-time partner, the great Regency architect John Nash, produced a stream of them for his clients – many of them, in fact, probably designed by Repton's sons, John Adey and George Stanley, who worked for many years in Nash's office. We also know from the few remaining letters from Nash to clients that he took their design and their relationship with settings very seriously and could argue as eloquently as Repton on the subject of Picturesque design.

From George Repton's notebooks, which date over the period of his employment in the Nash office, it is clear that he spent a great deal of time sketching vernacular cottages – almost certainly some of them from nature. The Nash office was probably one of the most productive sources of vernacular cottage design. It turned out vernacular cottages for landowners all over the country, but particularly in the West of England – for George Legh in Cheshire, John Edwards in Wales, John Matthews in Hereford,

A sketch from the
notebook of George
Stanley Repton
during the time he
worked for John
Nash. Essays in
deliberate vernacular
design are sometimes
difficult to
differentiate in the
notebook from
sketches from real
life. This shows a
cottage for George
Legh in Cheshire.

probably Lord Berwick at Attingham, and William Cooke and George Ward on the Isle of Wight, near Nash's own East Cowes Castle. And a number of the first designs for the Regent's Park villages appear to have been in a vernacular style.

These were not, as were many of the cottage styles in the hands of other later architects, simply churned out according to a decorative formula, for we know that Nash concerned himself with the relationship between his cottage buildings and their setting quite as much as he did for far grander and more lucrative commissions. It is clear that he was completely acquainted with the theoretical bases of the Picturesque and used them in practice and as the foundation for his explanations to clients about his design proposals.

The Nash office was also to design a vernacular cottage for the Picturesque founding father Uvedale Price at Foxley. It took the form of an irregular timber-framed cottage complete with diagonal strapwork and with various single-storey rooms and an open porch attended around a two-storeyed main section with clipped gables, paired chimneys and a thatched roof. And it is not impossible, given the close connections of the people involved in the Picturesque controversies, that it was also responsible for the cottage of one of the other fathers of Picturesque theory, Richard Payne Knight, although,

Built vernacular cottage by the Nash office for George Ward near East Cowes Castle, Isle of Wight: 'natural' rough stone construction, decorative slate roof, deliberately complicated arrangement of masses.

since Knight had designed his own castle in the 1770s, this may be by his own hand.

Knight not only wrote about the place of vernacular cottages in the Picturesque landscape but actually built one for himself. In around 1809, having given over Downton Castle to his heir, he built a cottage for himself in the grounds where, when he was not living in Soho Square in London, he lived the simple life, '... in as perfect happiness as my nature is capable of – wandering through romantic woods, planning and executing improvements every morning and enjoying my old books in undisturbed tranquillity every evening'.

It was a simple five-room cottage built, as he described it in a letter to Lord Aberdeen, '... of common masonry quite plain without any affection of rudeness [rusticity] ... or any way different from a common cottage of grey stone'.

The vernacular cottage style, its visual sources in both contemporary English landscape painting and that of the great seventeenth-century Low Country masters, the Nature-orientated thesis on which it was based: these are central to the other Picturesque styles. Its essence was that nature was the ultimate architectural guide, and its subsidiary themes were in praise of drawing on the architectural heritage of one's own national culture, of designing in harmony with Nature, the ultimate source of architecture – and in praise of Picturesque casualness of form, shape, materials and colour.

The earliest 'natural' cottage style was the Rustic. It is easily identified by its thatched roof (although now many have been re-roofed in cheaper slate or tile) with deep overhangs supported by a colonnade of rough timber tree-trunks and a few simple rooms underneath walled in the local material with door and window frames in the shape of pointed Gothic arches.

'Colonnade' is perhaps too grand a description for what was often enough a deep veranda at one end or around three sides. Most had a simple rectangular or circular plan, although slightly more complicated plans involving a combination of the two or the addition of bow fronts are common enough. In the cottage-book literature, architects conducted mild controversies about whether it was right to strip the bark off the 'columns' and whether to add branches in the form of rustic brackets at the top. A variety of reasons were advanced for the colonnade: 'The rude columns standing at a distance from the building form a kind of portico around it, casting a broad shadow and protecting the walls from bad weather,' said John Plaw. There are faint echoes here of Laugier's first man on that hot and unexpectedly showery day in the Arcadian glade. They looked rather self-consciously primitive, and the air of primitivism was what they were intended to convey.

Plaw's design, illustrated in his *Ferme Ornée* (1795) for a primitivist double cottage with rough tree-trunk veranda posts, simple thatched roof and Gothic windows.

Gunard Cottage, West Cowes, Isle of Wight. An early nineteenth-century vernacular cottage with stout tree-trunks supporting the porch and various additions attached in the approved Picturesque manner.

According to the designers, such as John Plaw, the most appropriate materials were '... thatch [which] may be of straw, reeds, rushes, etc ... and the external appearance of rough stucco or roughcast' – in keeping with the shaggy 'natural' theme.

Plaw himself published several books of designs based on the rustic cottage theme which varied in size from one-room shacks to villas. In practice most rustic cottages were rather small, two- or three-room single-storey dwellings, although it is not uncommon to find dormers to bedrooms in the roofspace peeping out from the thatch, and two-storey rustic cottages were built – one such with a two-storey colonnade was to be found near the back gate of East Cowes Castle, Isle of Wight, probably based on a similar design to be found in one of John Plaw's books of the 1790s. And the Prince Regent's Windsor Cottage was effectively a vast rambling collection of rustic cottages strung together.

There were, of course, many variations on the basic theme – all of them, however, retaining the basic simplicity of form and detail. Shadwell Park in Norfolk, for example, has at least five rustic cottages scattered around the estate and two rather larger house-sized cottages with thatched front verandas and bracketed timber posts – they look rather artificial because they lack the scale and simplicity of the others.

Primitivist circular cottage at Newbury, Berks. Originally this probably had rough timber veranda posts.

There is a remarkable consistency of style right across Britain from the now-demolished Newbury Lodge in Berkshire to Costessey Park in Norfolk and Gunard on the Isle of Wight. It was a very popular style simply because it was easy to do and because of its readily understood symbolism. Any landowner with a builder could design and build this kind of cottage because of its small size and simplicity of construction: a couple of rooms with a big thatch roof. The veranda posts could be cut from local trees, and small branches attached to form rustic brackets. With the addition of diamond-pattern windows and, often, pointed gothic door or window heads, the cottage was complete.

There were, of course, variations on the basic theme. Veranda posts could be stripped and traditional climbing plants such as ivy or woodbine trained around the rough, bare poles. The veranda could take different forms; walls could be plain brickwork or, more commonly, rough plastered or rendered; there could be dormers or not. All this meant that practically anybody could design and build such a cottage. And in some cases, where owners had higher architectural pretentions, the rustic forms could be tidied up to take the shape of a primitive Doric temple, for it was conventional wisdom that the characteristic details of the early Greek Doric temple were directly derived from timber constructions – and it was by working backwards through the supposed history of the earliest buildings from the temple that the conventional idea of the primitive hut had been developed.

There is a series of sketches by John Soane, the great Neoclassic architect of the early nineteenth century, for a dairy at Hamels. The earliest are for a simple rustic twiggy structure but, by a process of refinement which can be followed in succeeding drawings, Soane eventually decided on a rather Doric structure in which the vestiges of his earliest Primitivist intentions are only just visible. A similar progression from rustic to Neoclassical can be followed in the notebooks of the artist J.M.W. Turner. Sandicombe Lodge, his house on the Thames, is a fairly ordinary Regency building, with rather sparse Neoclassical details, but his original idea was to have a primitive rustic house – an idea which over several years was refined and architecturalized into the final version.

More prosaically, this cheap-and-cheerful style was also a grown-up, full-size version of those root-and-branch hermitages and primitive garden huts to be found in English landscapes of the second half of the eighteenth century. Part of a garden's stock of visual associations with Nature, this kind of structure was normally based more or less loosely on illustrations in architectural books of that time, from William Wright's charming little *Grotesque Architecture* of 1769, which actually contained designs for rustic garden buildings, through Sir William Chambers' *Civil Architecture* to contemporary editions of the first architectural book, *Ten Books on Architecture* by Vitruvius, which contained explanations and illustrations of the evolution of architecture from its primitive origins to the early stage of 'real' Greek architecture. Chambers, not entirely coincidentally, was the leading innovator in the development of the English Garden.

A rustic garden structure from William Wright's *Grotesque Architecture* (1769) – actually described by Wright as a primitive hut.

By the end of the century the French and other Europeans had regularly been building this kind of structure full size, although their interiors tended to be laid out as places for the entertainment of strollers through the garden. But in England the primitive hut style began to be used in a practical, functional way, for what was different about these full-size early nineteenth-century primitive rustic cottages was that they were intended to be inhabited by estate workers. They combined ornament with usefulness – the practical function of housing estate workers in new and more or less comfortable dwellings.

J.B. Papworth pointed out their Primitivist origins thus: 'The architects of the present day, attempting to combine fitness and beauty in rural buildings, revert to practices in the infancy of art, and forming their designs upon these simple models gain some advantage by the association of ideas in the minds of spectators.' The bonus in terms of social 'engineering' was that this association of ideas emphasized and reinforced the 'primitive' social state of the peasant inhabitants.

Cottages in the Rustic style were built well into the second half of the nineteenth century, but they did not really have the blessing of the Picturesque. Back at the beginning of the century Richard Payne Knight, one of the leading influences on the development of the theory, had warned about this kind of artificiality in typically cutting fashion: 'Rustic lodges to parks, dressed cottages, pastoral seats, gates and gateways made of unhewn

Cottage at Hawley's
Corner, Kent.

branches and stems of trees, have all necessarily a still stronger character of affectation; the rusticity of the first being that of a clown in a pantomime, and the simplicity of the others that of a shepherdess in a French opera. The real character of every object of this kind must necessarily conform to the use to which it is really appropriated and if attempts be made to give it any other character it will prove in fact to be only a character of imposture.'

With these strictures in mind – and the fact that the Rustic style was really only appropriate for very small buildings – architects soon began to elaborate on the basic theme. In properly irregular Picturesque fashion they incorporated some of its characteristic elements, such as thatch and rough veranda posts and rough walling finishes, into a style for larger cottages which was soon known as the cottage ornée.

———— •◆• ————

CHAPTER THREE

Hermitage for a Gentleman: The Cottage Ornée and the Old English Cottage

In many respects the cottage ornée was the upmarket version of the primitive rustic cottage. 'Though humble in its appearance it affords the necessary conveniences for persons of refined manners and habits,' explained Richard Pocock, introducing his book of cottage ornée designs in 1807.

But there were some very important additional elements apart from scale and class of occupant. It had, first of all, a deliberately complicated shape, form, texture and plan. There was the characteristic thatch, but it was likely to be in the form of a set of roofs joined and angled together into a complicated and irregular silhouette, often with eyebrow eaves, curly carved bargeboards, dormer windows and highly decorative chimneys poking through the summit. Instead of a few rooms neatly arranged underneath, there was a plan of often considerable complexity which was echoed on the outside by a rambling irregularity, freedom of form and selection of materials which, a few years before, in the eighteenth century, would have been unthinkable from the drawingboard of an architect who wanted to be taken seriously.

It is not as if the description 'cottage ornée' itself was all that serious. It is, of course, a made-up term and was probably invented by Robert Lugar, the great exponent of cottage ornée design. At all events, he was first to use it in print in 1805, and it soon became part of the language despite an attempt two years later by Richard Pocock to clean up the suspect term with the more correct 'cabane ornée'. As it happens, the French already used the term *chaumier* (and the Germans *Strohhütte*) for ornamental rustic buildings in their English Gardens. The British prefer their own variants on French language and grammar, and so 'cottage ornée' stuck. It belongs to the same etymological family as the term 'ferme ornée'. Equally a made-up term, this had been used since the middle of the eighteenth century to describe working farms which were also landscape gardens – such as Phillip Southcote's Wooburn Farm and Shenstone's Leasowes. Like the early nineteenth-century cottages ornées, they combined practicality with decorativeness.

Two T.F. Hunt designs in *Designs for Parsonage Houses, Almshouses etc.* (1827). In the foreground a cottage in the Old English style for an estate bailiff and (on the left) a rustic cottage ornée for an upper estate worker – the hierarchy in social caste is defined by style.

That is not to say that the cottage ornée was not intended to be taken with the utmost seriousness, but it was a different kind of seriousness from that of the past. The cottage ornée's design should, said Pocock, be '... calculated for comfort and convenience without minute attention to the rules of art, every part having its use apparent and the appearance in no way sacrificed to regularity [strict symmetry] ... every other part must appear conducive to this one end ... the comfort and convenience of its inhabitants'.

There are clear echoes here of James Malton's instruction to design the plan first to suit the owners and let the exterior shape and form follow on from that. That was a radical departure from Georgian architecture, which was primarily about conforming to a grammar of ornament and form rather than the livability of a dwelling.

At the same time, starting off from a practical rather than theoretical design premise allowed the designers of cottages ornées a tremendous freedom in what they could do with the appearance of their cottages. A design for a cabane ornée by Pocock of 1807, for example, combines some primitive rustic elements in the form of rough tree-trunk veranda posts

W.F. Pocock's design for a cabane ornée in his 1807 *Designs*. The design is firmly in the irregular Picturesque mode but the name never caught on.

supporting the eaves of a thatched roof with an eyebrowed dormer above. To one side is a large glazed conservatory and at the other a thatched porch with rough timber columns complete with timber capitals, in a (probably ironic) rough timber imitation of a classical Doric porch. Tiny twin gothic windows form a purely decorative addition to the chimneybreast, which is half concealed by climbing plants. A point of some interest in this slightly gauche composition is that Pocock has chosen to illustrate the *side* of the building rather than the front: the new cottage architecture was about dwellings as three-dimensional elements in the landscape rather than façade plus plain sides and back.

Robert Lugar's best published examples of the genre are Rose Hill Cottage at Marlow and Puckaster Cottage on the Isle of Wight. The former was a relatively large house made up of masses grouped casually together with tall chimneys breaking through the thatched roofs and forming a vital element in the composition. At the front door is a *porte cochère* with a gothic front and to one side a rustic thatched veranda wrapping around the lower part of a big two-storey bow. In the background a wood hangs close to the back of the cottage.

Puckaster Cottage is several years on in Lugar's architectural output from the Marlow cottage and, as Lugar tells us, is a deliberate development of it. Gone is the slightly tricksy gothic *porte cochère*, and in its place is a simple

Cottages at Blaise Hamlet, designed by John Nash for J.S. Harford at Blaise Castle. Astonishingly mature and dynamic three-dimensional compositions designed before the ink was dry on Picturesque theoretical writing.

and almost vernacular enclosed entrance porch with curly timber bargeboarding. The big bow of the earlier design with its wrap-around veranda has been simplified by putting the upper rooms into the big thatched roofspace and giving them dormers. Meanwhile climbing plants festoon the timber veranda posts, and plants and shrubs merge the lower parts of the walls into the surrounding lawn. It is not only a delightful composition, sitting low on its platform in front of the dramatic background of the Isle of Wight's Undercliff, but a very mature exercise in handling the new, irregular, complicated Picturesque design.

These two designs are contemporary with the Picturesque cottage ornée village at Blaise Hamlet – the unsurpassed model for dozens of imitations, the epitome of Picturesque grouping and designed with the assurance of an architect of very considerable imagination and understanding of his art.

Uvedale Price had written a considerable passage about the design of Picturesque villages and at Blaise Nash gave reality to these principles of design. Wrote Price: 'The characteristic beauties of a village are intricacy, variety and play of outline.... The houses should therefore be disposed with that view, and should differ as much in their disposition from those of a regularly built city, as the trees, which are meant to have the character of natural groups, should from those of an avenue.'

Blaise Hamlet was built for J.S. Harford, a Bristol magnate who had bought the estate some time before and had called in Humphry Repton to redesign the landscape. Repton had introduced a number of buildings in his landscape proposals – including the vernacular woodman's cottage (illustrated in the previous section) and a cottage ornée style dairy at the side of the house. The Nash-Repton partnership had, however, broken up by the time Harford decided to erect a village for old retainers, and Nash, who still employed the two Repton sons in his office, got the job.

Blaise consists of ten cottages grouped in a casual (in fact, very carefully organized) array around a village green. Variously thatched and stone slated, with dovecote gables, porches and seats, with rough stone walls and surmounted by clustered chimneys of a most extraordinarily elaborate kind, the whole ensemble nestled in a clearing in the wood opposite the castle's entrance gate. Each of the houses was an irregular assemblage of roofs and eaves and comfortable shaggy shapes – now carefully overgrown with creepers and plants. It made an extraordinary impression at the time, was illustrated on many occasions and was to remain the inspiration for all Picturesque village designers thereafter. The difficulty subsequent architects had was that Nash had effortlessly got it right first time.

Lugar and Nash – and Repton as well – were the great exponents of the style, but they had many imitators in builders and minor architects around

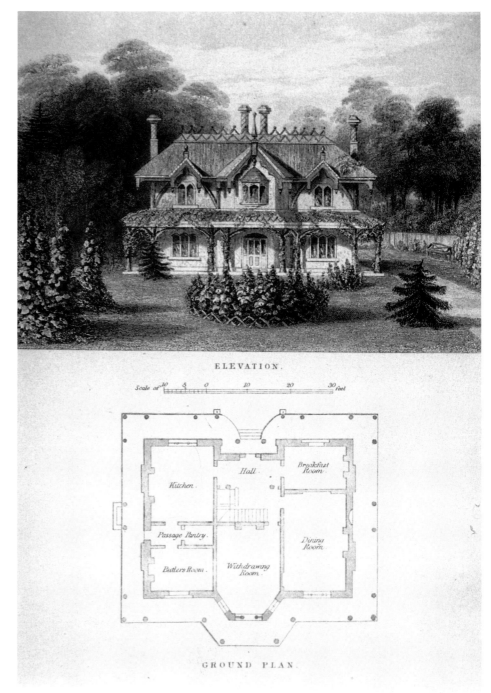

ELEVATION.

GROUND PLAN.

A cottage ornée in Richard Brown's *Domestic Architecture*, rather late in the style's history and, since the plan is rigidly symmetrical, decorative rather than Picturesque.

Cottage in Badminton village whose unknown designer has followed the Picturesque advice to emphasize irregularities of plan and form and to design as a three-dimensional object rather than as a brick box with a regular pattern of windows and doors on the sides and a roof on top.

the country. The little village at Badminton, for example, has two delightful cottage ornées – now incongruously and quite unpicturesquely located in the middle of the village street. The fashionable Decimus Burton, architect of the Traveller's Club in Pall Mall and of a number of the Regent's Park terraces and villas, had a particular affection for the style. He had used its simpler form, the rustic cottage style, for the animal houses at the London Zoological Gardens and continued to use the cottage ornée style for humans throughout his career, long after architects had given it up as unfashionable: at Beulah Spa, now a south London suburb, at Tunbridge Wells, at Furze Hill and elsewhere. Even his own bachelor home at St Leonards was in a tidied-up version of the style.

In the end the cottage ornée was satisfying as an experiment in incorporating nature into architecture, but it was not necessarily an experiment in integrating or incorporating architecture into nature – which is what the Picturesque at its best was about. However charming as designs they were, their naturalism was self-conscious. With their shaggy, irregular thatch, diamond-paned windows, porches and the occasional tree-trunk veranda columns, they were rather more symbolic of an association with nature – a somewhat crude attempt to imitate its forms rather than its qualities – than an attempt to consider seriously the problem of designing for the spirit of a place.

The Old English Domestic style began to be popular among cottage-designers in the 1820s. It was essentially a development of the Picturesque vernacular cottage style. At its best, said leading designer in the style P.F. Robinson, it was '… highly picturesque. The high pointed gable, the mullioned window and weathered chimney harmonise most agreeably in scenic situations and produce effects of high interest to the painter.' And in practice that is what the published Old English Domestic designs of the 1830s looked like: irregular Picturesque plans with gable roofs and decorative bargeboards, jettied, overhanging upper floors, tall decorative chimneys, diamond-pattern windows, half timbering and semi-dressed stonework – essentially the basic vernacular cottage with a sharper, more deliberately architectural quality in the form of 'characteristic' medieval details. As T.F. Hunt was to point out, 'The Picturesque in architecture does not belong exclusively to ruinous and useless hovels, but … it may be produced in newly-erected and comfortable houses.'

Old English cottage by P.F. Robinson in *Designs for Lodges and Park Entrances* (1833): massive decorative bargeboard, jettied upper floor, Gothic door and window heads.

Old English cottage in T.F. Hunt's *Half a Dozen Hints* (1825): curly bargeboards, jettied upper floor, elaborate chimney stacks, diamond-patterned windows and a flat Gothic arch over the entrance door.

In many ways it was simply a more architecturally upmarket version of the vernacular cottage plus added quasi-medieval decorations and details. They were 'quasi' because at the time remarkably little was known about real medieval cottage building and even less about its details and decoration. Almost all the evidence was literary. T.F. Hunt, author of a number of books of Old English Domestic cottage designs, conceded this: 'Time and the desolating wars ... have left us with a few traces of the habitations of that period ... All the writers, however, who speak of the subject agree that the houses of the great were more magnificent than comfortable, and that the lower orders were miserably lodged.' That was not much to go on, although local lore at the time held that one old bailiff's house, the Grange at Whalley near Manchester, was an authentic surviving example of a small pre-Tudor house.

On the other hand, the lack of precise knowledge about medieval cottage-detailing meant that architects designing in the Old English Domestic style could do more or less what they pleased. And that was entirely in accordance with mainstream Picturesque thinking, which said that it was ridiculous, or at least incongruous, to attempt to copy exactly the architecture of the past in modern buildings. 'The scale of its exactitude becomes that of its incongruity, and the deviation from principle, proportioned to the fidelity of imitation,' said leading theorist Richard Payne

Knight. It needs to be said that Old English Domestic designers were not entirely put off by that – or by the lack of authentic details to copy. They were, after all, introducing a new style and in marshalling their arguments in its favour needed a certain amount of traditional authority for what they were doing.

Several cottage books of the 1830s included sections illustrating decorative timber fragments from remaining medieval buildings, and T.F. Hunt's *Exemplars of Tudor Architecture*, a bookful of these kinds of details 'selected from modern edifices', was an attempt to establish himself as something of an authority on medieval building – and thus on new Old English Domestic cottage design. It was also a crib book for contemporary Old English designers.

All this was in line with a growing interest in early nineteenth-century Britain in archaeology and in Gothic architecture. Until publication of the results of the laborious recording of medieval churches by members of the Cambridge Camden Society later in the century, it was all to be pretty crude stuff – and naïve: for example, it was long assumed that the Gothic style in churches and cathedrals was a uniquely English invention despite what now seems to be the self-evidence of its importation from Europe by masons and religious orders.

A further reason for this little interest in archaeological exactness was the need to distinguish Old English from Modern Gothic – which was, in the eyes of the new cottage medievalists, no more than a matter of tacking on Gothic details such as pointed windows and arches, pinnacles, finials and battlements to otherwise very ordinary buildings. As E.B. Lamb was to say in the late 1850s, 'At the time of its being introduced and adopted into modern practice, so very ill was our medieval architecture understood ... that notwithstanding its evident and almost total unfitness for the purpose, the ecclesiastical style of former times was ... mistaken as one for [domestic] architecture.'

One of the attractions of Old English Domestic was the fact that it was British through and through. Cottage-book author P.F. Robinson wrote solemnly about his high purpose of 'restoring a style peculiar to this country'; T.F. Hunt attempted to engage his readers in the idea that, 'English Architecture is still the most applicable for English habitation'; and other writers spoke about the style as one 'which may be said to be indigenous to this soil' and 'better suited to the scenery of this country'. These were presumably thought to be powerful arguments for the style in a country which was recently liberator of Europe, owner of a large section of the planet and just launching into the heady future of the Industrial Revolution.

One of the Old English vernacular dwellings on the green at Ockley, Surrey. Here rather more vernacular with mixed stone-and-brick walling and exuberant decoration all arranged in a picturesque group of masses and roofs.

Humphry Repton, the great Picturesque landscape designer, had designed probably the first recorded vernacular cottage, and he was also years ahead of popular Old English cottage-designers. His Old English (strictly speaking Tudor) style Apsley Wood Lodge still stands at a northern entrance to the Duke of Bedford's Woburn Abbey estate. Designed and built in the early part of the second decade of the nineteenth century, this perfectly detailed little dwelling embodies Picturesque vernacular: a gabled two-storey block in the middle flanked unequally on either side by single-storey wings, one of whose roofs shelters an open porch at the front. A tall, splendidly elaborate chimneystack rises from one side of the main block, providing a visual pivot or focus for the composition. The Old English element consists of the detailing: the decorative bargeboards, the slightly jettied upper floor with diamond-paned windows and ogival tracery at the tops. Some of the external walls are in stone, some in brick nogging and some in half timbering. Timber finials crown the gable ends – and were originally repeated on the nearby gateposts. On the other side of the gate, which was part of the whole design, was to be found a little formal garden in the Tudor style. Here was not simply a pleasant little Picturesque cottage design simply dropped into a picturesque setting, for Repton had also composed the design of its immediate surroundings as well.

The Reptons' design for Apsley Wood Cottage, Woburn Park. On one level an exercise in antiquarianism in which each component in the composition has a traceable source yet in practice is a sure visual composition.

Repton had earlier written against 'professed antiquarians' but his client, the Duke of Bedford, had quite specifically asked him for a lodge in the style of domestic buildings erected before the reign of Henry VIII. The Duke had hit on this fairly arbitrary date not because he had any special knowledge of the period or because of any special associations it had for him: it was simply because he detested the contemporary Modern Gothic cottage style with its tacked-on cardboardy church gothic detailing. Specifying the style in this fashion avoided that possibility.

As it happened, Repton's son John, an architectural assistant in the office of John Nash and himself an experienced designer of vernacular cottages, had developed an interest in archaeology and was later to publish several important texts on the subject. On this occasion the father and son teamed up to take advantage of the Duke's specification about date literally, for each detail in this lodge cottage has a traceable source. The vertical brick nogging is taken from a medieval timber house at Lyme Regis, the stone plinth around the base of the cottage from a building near Eltham Palace, the front door from a house near Sudbury in Suffolk, the chimneystack from Wolterton Manor and so on. Even the plan and selection of plants for the little garden were based on studies of Tudor paintings, and the original paintwork on the gate and its fence were from a similar source.

The Old English cottage style in reality at Wakehurst Place, Surrey – here organized symmetrically around the front porch.

When Repton published this design in his 1816 *Fragments and Hints on Landscape Gardening*, he spelled out the provenance for each of these and the other details in uncharacteristically careful fashion. It was uncharacteristic because Repton usually preached in favour of impressionism rather than obsessively accurate detail. The internal evidence suggests that it was all intended as a little boost to his deaf son's personal reputation as a designer and antiquarian. On the other hand, because it was published and because it was published by the influential Repton, this somewhat fancifully elaborate antiquarianizing encouraged later Old English Domestic designers to follow suit.

The most amusing outcomes of all this were two much later lodge cottages at Barn Hall, Buckinghamshire. In the 1880s Lord Burnham cased two of his irregularly shaped lodges in genuine old English wood-carving, gradually incorporating and adding sections of panelling as they came to hand. The result is dramatic and rather curious because on close inspection much of the panelling is clearly from interiors – and much of it surely carefully aged modern work. If Burnham failed in creating much in the way of authenticity, he splendidly succeeded in giving his visitors a pastiche taste of the spirit of archaeology first raised by the Reptons.

Repton's Apsley Wood lodge had more immediate influences on cottage design, for it showed that it was possible to evoke the indigenous British

Cottage in an Old English style at Thornham Parva, West Suffolk: brickwork in diaper pattern, 'half timbering', heavy bargeboards and an irregular, Picturesque form.

architectural past with a degree of success. It was, to use his own, impossible-to-verify words, '...a tolerably fair specimen of the style and size of private houses three hundred years ago ... [when] some of the dwelling houses of respectable persons did not much exceed this cottage in dimensions or comfort, when one living room was often deemed sufficient for all the family'.

This was the problem faced by any cottage stylist: the fact that the original models were not suited to contemporary patterns and standards of life. Architects were torn between emphasizing that their designs looked like traditional 'medieval' cottages – or at least gave people the impression of having medieval associations – and emphasizing the practicality and comfort of the interiors. Most tried to do both. Hunt, for example, in a passage which went straight back to Repton's detailed explanation of the sources for his Apsley Wood lodge a decade earlier, declared that his purpose was to '...bring together some of the forms and decorations of the Old Rural Architecture which are now only to be seen in detatched parts and scattered widely abroad – and to apply them to plans formed upon modern principles of construction, convenience and comfort'.

P.F. Robinson, Francis Goodwin and T.F. Hunt are best remembered as leading exponents of the Old English style simply because they published so much about it. But it was a popular style for any architect with a client susceptible to Picturesque principles and who was not averse to giving the impression that his estate was rather older than it was. For installing a gate

Cottage at a side
entrance to
Barn Hall,
Buckinghamshire,
*c.*1880. An exercise
in almost obsessive
antiquarianism in
which old reclaimed
timber detailing has
been attached to a
basic brick structure
to produce a
Picturesque form.

Detail of panelling on
the main lodge to
Barn Hall with what
looks remarkably like
sections of old or
perhaps recarved
interior panelling.

Lodge gate to Great Bounds Park, Kent: elaborate Old English in a manner reminiscent of some of P.F. Robinson's designs.

lodge and cottage or two in the Old English style, whatever else their visual and cultural virtues, was a way of giving a newly bought estate the air of venerable and respectable age.

The Old English style was a very close cousin to the vernacular style of cottage. It was a revival of a distinctly uncertain building tradition, a clearly apposite vehicle for deploying Picturesque principles of design, the domestic parallel to the Gothic Revival in church and public building design – and the architectural parallel to the Old English historical romances of such writers as Sir Walter Scott. The Old English style struck a long and resonant chord among architects and their clients alike. For the rest of the century it was to be the accepted style for domestic architecture.

CHAPTER FOUR

---·---

Home of the Noble Savage: The Swiss Cottage

The name 'Swiss Cottage' is well known because a Swiss cottage-style public house, built by Meux the brewers in the 1840s, gave its name to a north London locality. But not very many seem to have been built. Writing in the late 1830s, the architect Richard Varden laid claim to authorship of most of those which had: 'With the exception of those I have erected, I do not remember having seen above three or four true Swiss buildings in the kingdom … no doubt there are many others, but they have not come under my observation.'

Varden himself had probably built only a few – at Powick and at Cheltenham in Gloucestershire, and his contemporary E.B. Lamb designed one at around the same time for John Murrary's estate near Stranraer in Scotland. Yet Varden had conveniently ignored the existence of a series of well-known Swiss cottage designs in various cottage books by P.F. Robinson dating from the early 1820s. He had also designed the set of Swiss rooms in the Colosseum Regent's Park in 1832 which contemporary reviewers found particularly evocative. Robinson had the advantage of having actually gone to Switzerland in 1816 – as soon as it was possible to travel abroad after the Napoleonic Wars, and he claimed a degree of authenticity for his designs thereby.

Although there are no known Robinson-designed Swiss cottages in existence, he may have been the author of the now-demolished Swiss cottage at Bulstrode Park, Bucks, and of that at Cassiobury Park, Herts, which still remains. But there were other architects working in the style as well, including the contemporary cottage-book writer Francis Goodwin. In 1833 Jeffrey Wyattville, the Prince Regent's favourite architect, had designed and constructed one for the Duke of Bedford at Endsleigh, Devon, in the form of a two-storeyed structure with a deep veranda around three sides and rough vertical boarding covering the walls. There were said to have been several on the Isle of Wight by the late 1820s, and J.B. Papworth published several Swiss or Polish designs in Ackermann's *Repository of Arts, Literature and*

Swiss cottage by P.F. Robinson published in his *Ornamental Villas* (1872). The gaucheness of the design may be due to the fact that Robinson had made sketches in Switzerland and had given a priority over composition to accurate rendition of interesting features he had observed.

Swiss cottage at Cassiobury Park, Herts., one of a number of Picturesque regional cottages in the park.

Fashion in 1819. One of these designs indicates another origin for the Swiss Cottage, which was less to do with Picturesqueness than with imitating the Swiss and Polish and Russian *chaumiers* to be found in pre-Revolutionary French gardens — garden stage-sets in the form of cottages and farmlets of which Marie Antoinette's Hameau was the best-known example. Perversely the Hameau was supposed to have been an imitation of a vernacular *English* village.

Papworth's design was not original: he had taken it from a collection of illustrations of these European garden buildings published by J.C. Krafft in Paris in 1809 and 1810. The French *chaumier* was well known in Britain before this: a reviewer of James Malton's *British Cottage Architecture* had criticized the author for not having said anything about '... the Swiss Cottage or *chaumier* from which we think ideas may be adopted with effect in this country'.

Malton would certainly not have agreed but later architects and commentators were to see some Picturesque possibilities in the style. The traveller James Cockburn wrote about the real Swiss hut from the painter's point of view: he thought that their '... forms are perfectly picturesque and seem to court the pencil to portray them, their large broad gables and flat roofs overhang the walls, the sides half wood with the foundations of stone; penthouses, chimneys and exterior staircases ... cannot fail to please the painter's eye.'

The problem faced by hard-line Picturesque designers was getting the right relationship between the cottage and its surroundings. Varden, writing about his published cottage designs, noted that one had been carefully sited on a bank overlooking a deep road cutting: 'A suitable situation is of great importance to a Swiss cottage, but such may generally be found in an undulating, and always hilly country. The edge of a steep bank whether natural or artificial is very appropriate. The slopes of railway cuttings and embankments are features that point out this style as suitable for small station houses, if quite in the country.' (It hardly needs to be said that this was the beginning of the great railway-building era.) And a contemporary, 'Professor' William Brown, in an otherwise absurdly pompous book of cottages and villas in every style imaginable, actually named areas in his native Devon and Cornwall which he thought sufficiently dramatic and appropriate for Swiss cottages — Torquay, Babbacombe and Ilfracombe among them.

A more sceptical view was that there were really not many suitable settings for the Swiss Cottage in the relatively flat and rolling English countryside. W.H. Leeds, the architectural commentator in Francis Goodwin's cottage book of the mid 1830s, criticized one of Goodwin's more imaginatively

GEOMETRICAL ELEVATION OF A DESIGN FOR A SWISS COTTAGE,

AS AN ENTRANCE TO A PARK.

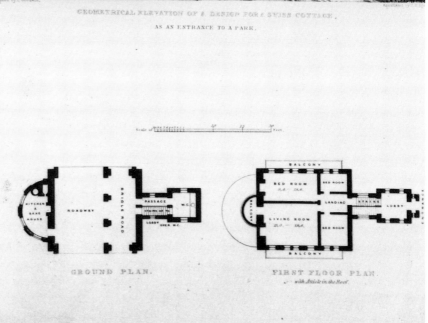

GROUND PLAN.

FIRST FLOOR PLAN.

with Attick in the Roof.

Swiss lodge published by Francis Goodwin in his *Domestic Architecture* (1834): described by a commentator as 'un-English' on the grounds that it would be difficult to find such rugged topography in England. The Italianate tower on the right is presumably a reference to Switzerland's proximity with Italy – and perhaps the interconnections between European vernacular styles.

Picturesque Swiss cottage designs, arguing that it would hardly be '... generally applicable, since it would require a peculiar style of scenery sufficiently mountainous, at least hilly, to justify so un-English a style'. J.C. Loudon was of the same opinion, because the English countryside had none of the terrific torrents, wild crags and aweful chasms of the Swiss cottage's original setting. But, thought Loudon, it might be justified on the grounds of 'character' – that is, that such a cottage in the appropriately rugged setting might raise up '... interesting associations in the mind of a continental traveller and fill the stationary inhabitants with surprise – and by exciting enquiry, might lead to the improvement of their taste'. Loudon was trying hard to find some justification for a cottage style for which he had little real enthusiasm.

As one might expect, most later Swiss cottages were built on relatively level sites.

There were other reasons for the vogue for the Swiss cottage – more perhaps as an idea than necessarily the kind of building a gentleman or landowner might actually want to build. For the Swiss, Swiss scenery and Swiss peasants were much in vogue in early nineteenth-century Britain. The struggle of this sturdy mountain people against the Austrians had struck a chord in the popular imagination in much the same way as various oppressed groups do in the world today. They appeared in poetry and literature and on the stage and, even if the plots of ostensibly Swiss dramas consisted of the unusual contrived duels, disguised lovers, abductions and the like common to bucolic stage plays about the artless peasant's Natural Life, the splendidly evocative stage scenery probably helped more than anything to fix the locale in the popular mind. 'The narrow streams, the rugged bridge that but feebly connects its steep banks, the peaked mountains, the intervening glaciers' to use the words of one enthralled critic of the 1794 production of *The Travellers in Switzerland* at Covent Garden – were probably much more realistic than the plot. This drama was but one of scores of plays with Swiss themes which were produced in London over the next decades.

The serious literature of the time, including that of Wordsworth and William Godwin, provided equally evocative visions. Wordsworth has a long passage about the Swiss scenery and the primitive life in the *Prelude*, where he talks about deep haunts and aboriginal vales,

> Quiet and lorded over and possessed
> By naked huts, wood built, and sown like tents
> Or Indian cabins over the fresh lawn.

And a major section of Godwin's *Fleetwood* is set in the Alps, to which his eponymous hero has fled to find peace from the turmoils of vicious London society. There he finds similarities with other primitive settings: 'I felt as if I were in the wildest and most luxuriant of the uninhabited islands of the South Seas. I was lost in a vision of Paradise, of habitations and bowers among the celestial orbs … of the pure rewards and enjoyments of a better state.' Neither author had the faintest idea what the Noble Savage life of the Swiss, Amerinds or South Seas islanders was like: here they were suggesting in a rather flowery way that the Swiss belonged somehow to the genus Noble Savage, the universal Child of Nature who built his simple shelter from the materials of the Arcadian wood.

With this kind of respectable popular imagery available on the bookstalls and on the stage, it is not entirely surprising that the British should take some of it with them in their mind's eye when they started to travel abroad again after the Napoleonic Wars. Typical was Thomas Roscoe, who took the artist Samuel Prout on a sketching tour of the Alps in the early 1820s. He wrote about his first-hand experiences in predictably romantic Noble Savage terms: 'The habitations [like the peasantry] bear an appearance so perfectly primitive that one might with reason believe their architecture had known no alteration since the time when houses were constructed with no other earthly view than that of shelter.'

The Swiss cottage at the Duke of Bedford's Rustic Villa at Endsleigh, Devon by Jeffrey Wyattville: distinguishable as Swiss by its timber siding here laid vertically rather than horizontally, and a deep first-floor veranda.

Here were latter-day primitive huts in a latter-day Arcadian glade, and they offered themselves as attractive models for architects because they seemed authentically 'primitive' or at least more authentic than the rustic cottage whose symbolism was more serious than its historical accuracy. They also had the faint allure that anything foreign has, and it was easier to make up little Primitivist fantasies about buildings in foreign countries which were not likely to be visited by most people. It is clear from other writers of the time that it was the popular exposure of the Swiss and their primitive lives which focused the attention of architects towards the style – and doubtless encouraged clients at least to think about it as an option.

Despite all the emphasis on the Swiss, there was not thought to be much real difference between the styles of most of the northern European peasantry: they were for all intents and purposes the work of beings as close to the state of noble savagery as it was possible to get in the modern Western world. J.C. Loudon, for example, talked about a Swiss cottage design he had published in his *Encyclopaedia* as being of a style 'common to the northern parts of the continent of Europe and also Switzerland'. And elsewhere writers described the characteristic timber construction with overhanging first floors, overhanging eaves and gables, heavy timber bracketing and small shuttered windows as being anything from Swiss to Polish or Norwegian – and even Russian.

In that sense the Swiss Cottage was a special case of the vernacular cottage – in fact, somewhere between it and, say, the Old English (from which it often is difficult to distinguish in designs and in built examples). That is to say, it was Picturesque in visual terms but clearly marked as a special style by its characteristic shape and decoration.

But in the end it was not entirely satisfactory. The Old English and even the Modern Gothic were somehow naturalized to the soil of England. The Swiss Cottage, however vernacular, however intentionally 'unselfconscious', it was in the end alien to the culture and landscape of England.

CHAPTER FIVE

Villa Rustica: The Making of the Italian Vernacular Style

In the middle of this wave of vernacular cottage styles it is a little surprising to come across the Italian style – especially when the new cottage architecture had so abruptly turned its back on Italian classicalism. Yet the Italian cottage style was, like the Old English style, to become an immensely popular way of building cottages – and both were to be transformed, in a very simplified form, into the *de rigueur* styles for the new suburban architecture of Britain, the colonies and America in the late nineteenth century. By then they had lost their Picturesque roughness and informality and had become almost as much a formula style as had the old Georgian domestic architecture of the eighteenth century.

In fact, the Italian cottage style was Picturesque *par excellence* – and for special reasons. First of all, it was not classical Italian but Italian *vernacular*, despite the fact that here and there might be found the occasional classical motif such as a pilaster, architrave or moulding. They were understood as either the fragments of an old classical building which had been incorporated *ad hoc* into a peasant building or as bastard-classical details which had gradually been corrupted and over-simplified over the centuries by the hand of untutored builders. Italy was a special case because the remains of its two-millennia-old civilization were still highly visible. That meant that the standard vernacular argument had to be slightly modified to take into account the fact that in Italy vernacular architecture could not entirely avoid a highly traditional architectural past.

The second special quality about Italian vernacular buildings was that they figured in the landscape paintings of the seventeenth-century artists Claude Lorraine and Nicholas and Gaspar Poussin – greatly admired paintings which were the recommended models for Picturesque composition. It was not, said Picturesque theory, that these vernacular buildings and decaying farmhouses should be slavishly imitated – rather that the way the great landscape masters had portrayed this kind of building offered the landscape

Claude Lorraine's *Pastoral Landscape with the Ponte Mollo* (etched by Richard Earlom for his *Liber Veritatis*, 1787). Claude frequently included vernacular farmhouse buildings in his landscapes.

and architectural designer a guide as to how he should compose his own designs.

Furthermore, Picturesque theory approved of the 'mixed' styles which were to be found in those paintings – buildings which looked as though they had been built and then added to here and there and modified over a long period of time. J.B. Papworth was to design a large Picturesque cottage – in fact, rather more the size of a villa – along these lines, incorporating a variety of Italianesque forms vaguely reminiscent of buildings to be seen in the Poussins' paintings to create a rural home and studio for – who else than a landscape painter. Comparisons between building and painting strongly suggest that when years before, in around 1804, John Nash had built Cronkhill, the home of the steward for Attingham Park, he used Claude Lorraine's painting *Landscape with the Ponte Mollo* as a visual source for this extraordinarily accomplished early example of Picturesque villa design.

In practice, of course, it was easier for architects to go ahead and design vaguely Italian details and forms, and to make a show of calling on the Italian landscape masters as precedent, especially when architects wanted to introduce novel Italianate features into the British countryside. Thus P.F. Robinson argued for the incorporation of bell towers or lookout towers into

Italian villa in J.B. Papworth's *Rural Residences* (1818). An example of design by the accretion of architectural masses arranged knowingly to form a three-dimensional composition, and consciously modelled on landscape drawings and paintings by Claude Lorraine.

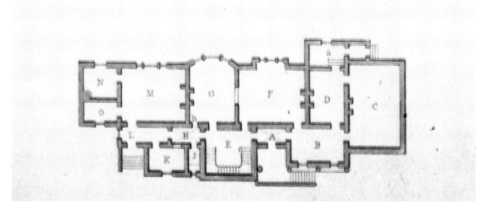

John Nash's Cronkhill, Attingham Hall, Shropshire of around 1805. A brilliant and very early study in three-dimensional massing has unmistakably drawn on Claudian landscape models – Earlom's book was in the Attingham library at the time of designing.

Italian cottages on the grounds that these were a feature frequently introduced 'in the work of the great Italian masters'.

For cottage-designers who were not familiar with the great collections of the seventeenth-century masters, there was Gilbert Laing Meason's curious 1828 crib book *On the Landscape Architecture of the Great Painters of Italy*. The greater part of this book contained etching of buildings and details singled out from the backgrounds of landscapes by such painters as Michelangelo, Raphael, Titian and, of course, the Poussins and Claude. They were intended by Meason to provide contemporary architects with visual inspiration, with lessons on the new irregular, dynamic composition (in place of the old orderliness and symmetry) and, occasionally, with models for direct imitation.

J.C. Loudon, the cottage encyclopaedist, was most impressed with the purpose of Meason's book and his selection of building examples. The new Picturesque design, Loudon pointed out, was particularly dependent on the designer's discrimination and judgement. These were acquired with difficulty, and Loudon earnestly exhorted the young architect to study Meason's plates carefully, 'endeavouring to discover the causes of the satisfaction they afford him'. An additional advantage, thought Loudon, was that many of these visual extracts might be converted into comfortable dwellings 'with very little alteration'. Loudon was never the man to allow high principle to affect what he saw as practical good sense.

Here then was a vernacular style whose authority was no less than the quintessentially Picturesque painting of the seventeenth century, whose models still stood in the Italian landscape (who knows, perhaps the very cottages painted by Claude Lorraine two centuries before), whose characteristic quality, said Loudon, '... may be given in two words – painterlike effect'.

A slightly more cynical view is that the introduction of the Italian vernacular style was a way of reconciling old-time supporters of the classical tradition with the new irregular and free approach to architecture – or, put another way, that Picturesque cottage designers thought it politic to absorb the Italian style into their repertoire in order to attract a broader spread of clients. That is one explanation for the curious introduction by T.F. Hunt, the Old English Domestic designer, to his 1827 *Architettura Campestre*, of a set of charming little Italian vernacular cottage designs. There he announced that his real purpose in publishing the designs was to '... do little more than render manifest the inferiority [of the Italian vernacular] to that beautiful and appropriate style miscalled gothic'. That did not stop him from actually publishing the designs. They were very popular – the book ran to four further editions: he understood his market.

Hunt was not the only Picturesque cottage-book author to stand in both camps. P.F. Robinson, in the middle of the 1820s, when the style really began to be popular, said he thought its features 'incompatible with the humble and retired existence of the cottager'. He was to go on to publish a large number of Italian cottage designs.

Robinson's designs have a considerable degree of authenticity because he had gone on a sketching tour in Italy and Europe in the early 1820s. He was one of a number of young architects who, once the Napoleonic Wars were over, had taken the opportunity to cross the Channel and undertake modest versions of the leisurely Grand Tours which eighteenth-century English *milordi* had made as the finishing touches to their education and which the occasional architect made, if he had the money or if he had won a Royal Academy Schools' travelling scholarship, in order to see and sketch at first hand the architectural monuments on which his own designs were founded.

European sketching tours were to become a familiar feature in the education of young nineteenth-century artists, writers and architects. Robinson had been preceded by the tireless investigator and collector of information John Claudius Loudon, and he was to be followed by such later architectural luminaries as Gilbert Scott, Charles Barry and George Basevi. Once there, as their notebooks show, they assiduously sketched and recorded pages full of Italian hillside villages, farmhouses, cottages and

Designs by Charles Parker for Italian cottages published in *Villa Rustica* between 1832 and 1834. Adaptations for the English peasantry of his Italian sketches of vernacular buildings.

scenery – as well as the standard classical remains. Theirs were more journeys of visual discovery than – as had been the case in the eighteenth century – confirmation of the essential rightness of the way to do architecture.

It was not, of course, only architects and artists who made these tours for from the time of Shelley, Keats and Browning in the early nineteenth century to the interwar poets and writers of the 1930s, Italy and the Italian tour were an essential feature of British literary and artistic life.

In the late 1820s the young architect Charles Parker undertook such a tour and on his return began to publish exquisite lithographs of vernacular houses and farmhouses set in delicate Claudian landscapes. In fact, they were designs, reworked from his on-the-spot sketches, for new Italian-style cottages complete with plans – and were intended for British settings. Eventually published together as the book *Villa Rustica*, they represent the high point in Italian Picturesque cottage-book publication. Evenly balancing the importance of landscape and buildings in proper Picturesque fashion and designed with consummate sureness, this collection of designs could scarcely fail to seduce the eye of a prospective builder.

Italian vernacular gatehouse to Court Lodge, Hunton, Kent, *c*.1835. The built reality was often more prosaic and simplified than the design idea.

Italian cottage at Trentham, Staffordshire probably by Charles Barry who designed the great house. In the translation from Italian farmhouse model to reality a great deal is lost – although the pantiles, commonly used in Italy were made locally.

Jeffrey Wyattville's design for one of the lodges adjacent to the Italianate village of Edensor at Chatsworth. J.C. Loudon, writing in 1836, described it, slightly unfairly, as a 'specimen of what, twenty years ago, was reckoned the Italian style'.

Real-life Italian vernacular style cottages in Britain turned out to be rather more prosaic. As we have seen, the Italian vernacular style probably appealed to those cottage-builders who were not completely convinced about abandoning every aspect of the age-old classical Italian tradition. It was also easy to design and build. Characteristically it was rather blocky and foursquare, and therefore was easy for a builder to set out. Its decorative details were simple: rafter-end brackets under the eaves, plain window surrounds, low-pitched tile or slate roofs, the odd square-column colonnade or porch and, often, a little tower. Where a local builder might have difficulties in getting completely right an elaborate cottage ornée or an Old English cottage, with their decorative carved bargeboards, strapwork half timbering and relatively complicated layout, the Italian style made fewer demands.

Other cottage-book architects could supply versions simpler than Parker's. For example, Hunt's designs were for cottages of not more than two or three rooms, and Robinson and his contemporary Francis Goodwin, who included a number of Italian vernacular cottages in their books, offered buildings of a similar size. The two idiosyncratic cottages at Alton Towers, based on designs in Hunt's *Architettura Campestre* are no more than two- or three-room cottages, although the stone Italian vernacular railway station of a later date at the entrance to the estate is a little more commodious.

Entrance lodge at Shrubland Park, Suffolk in an elaborate Italian style, vernacular only in the sense that this kind of thing was thought to be visible in the Italian countryside.

Italian cottage at the rear entrance to Shrubland Park. A back entrance lodge in the Italian farmhouse style.

At Trentham, the great Italianate house in Staffordshire, Charles Barry designed cottages round the back in a plain Italian vernacular style – complete with the local Staffordshire pantiles. And at the nearby Derbyshire great house Chatsworth, Jeffrey Wyattville designed two lodge gates for the entrance road, one in Italian vernacular, the other in Old English. Off to the side of these gates is the village of Edensor, a stone-built group of cottages and houses in a mixture of styles from Italian vernacular to vaguely Romanesque to Old English buildings: '…all the prettiest styles of cottage architecture from the sturdy Norman to the sprightly Italian,' said *The Gardener's Chronicle* in the early 1840s, not long after the village had been completed. It was a mixture of styles which Decimus Burton had put together at Calverly Park, a housing estate of small villas or large cottages at Tunbridge Wells, whose entrance lodge was in the by-then outdated cottage ornée style. Burton was no great purist in matters of style.

Perhaps the two most fascinating Italian-style cottages are at Shrubland Park. Clearly designed as low-style accompaniments to the Italian Classical of the house, they are to be found at the front and back gates to the estate. The Picturesque writers had pointed out that one of the ways of linking cottage styles and their surroundings was to pay attention to the style of architecture of the owner's house – it was part of the local scene as much as the natural landscape, so the front lodge to Shrubland Park has a modestly impressive arcaded loggia across the front, and a heavily quoined tower with single-storey blocks added on to either side. Nestling in its background of heavy planting, it provides the visitor with a comfortable visual clue to the splendours of the great house.

Even more interesting is the lodge at the back gate, for its mixture of formality, in the form of the slightly gauche colonnade across the front of a highly irregular main section, complete with little *campanile* (almost certainly a chimney). It is much more evocative of the Italian *campagna* and more comfortably Picturesque in its straggling irregularity.

Italian cottages continued to be built in relatively small numbers – usually where there was a case for architectural consistency with a mansion in the Italianate or the Italian classical style. It was a useful style for architects and clients who wanted to retain a vestige of the classical tradition and introduce the new Picturesque mode. But it was soon to be seen, much abbreviated and watered down, in the more elaborate suburban developments of cities – and in a much more attenuated version in the terrace-house developments which were filling out the cores of Britain's industrial towns and the expanding towns of the colonies in the New World.

CHAPTER SIX

Villages of Vision

Nash had revolutionized the design of villages with Blaise Hamlet. Its perfect Picturesque grouping, the woodland setting, and the way in which its individual cottages blended into the whole scene demonstrated that the Picturesque was not only a persuasive set of theoretical ideas but worked in practice. No architect for half a century and longer afterwards could have set pencil to paper without Blaise rising in his mind's eye. That could be inhibiting, because he knew that his peers understood the lessons of Blaise as well, so that direct imitation would be instantly detectable.

That was not to stop imitations – although, with a few exceptions, such as Holly Village in London's Highgate, they ended up half-hearted affairs, because either the client did not have enough money or the architect had insufficient imagination. Somerleyton village in East Anglia is one such case. The half Old English, half cottage ornée cottages with feeble strapwork are Picturesquely grouped around a village green in the Blaise fashion, but the spacing of the houses, their crude details and the looseness of the whole visual ensemble recall the warning Nash issued in a letter to one of his clients in 1798: 'In scattering cottages without any principle to go by, confusion instead of picturesque intricacy is often produced.'

Holly Village, on the other hand, designed by H.A. Darbyshire for the Baroness Burdett-Coutts in 1865, is a creditable re-creation of Blaise. The Baroness scandalized London society when in her sixties she married her thirty-year-old secretary. Her village, like Blaise, was built for elderly servants and, like Blaise fifty years before, the cottages were scattered carefully around a village green. Unlike Blaise, which the stroller used to come upon in the middle of a wood, Holly Village has an imposing entrance gate. The cottages are rather larger than those at Blaise and in a Gothic Revival rather than vernacular or cottage ornée style: pale yellow bricks, curly bargeboards, pointed windows and the occasional small tower. But with the extensive planting which has grown up around and over the cottages, the artificiality of the architecture is submerged and the village forms a

One of the vernacular cottages at Baldersby, Yorks.

fascinating Picturesque grouping in which the weakness of the individual parts is made up for by the effect of the whole. A contemporary described it all as '*villeggiatura*'.

A decade before, in the mid 1850s, the great Gothic Revival architect William Butterfield started building the new village of Baldersby St James surrounding his stunning Gothic Revival church. The village has the same kind of authenticity as the church, and without closer inspection it is easy to mistake for a real Yorkshire village. The vicarage, perhaps the one weak point in the design, is in a kind of squared-up cottage ornée manner with curly bargeboards and a fairly regular plan. Across the road is the schoolhouse, a Picturesque vernacular building similar to several other schools by Butterfield in the area, with steeply pitched roofs and the occasional section of half timbering in a fashion which James Malton would surely have approved. The villagers are housed in thatched and slated single and double cottages in the local, not very dramatic, Yorkshire brick. The further they are sited away from the church, the smaller they become – as did the importance of their inhabitants in the estate village pecking order. It is an arrangement which the Picturesque encyclopaedist John Claudius Loudon had recommended: 'Variety will be produced by a difference in accommodation and style of the cottages. The dwellings of the clergyman and of the schoolmaster will not only be larger than the others, but will have more land attached.'

Further south, in Derbyshire, in the 1830s Loudon's former drafting assistant William Robertson laid out a model village for the Chatsworth estate. Named Edensor, presumably a Primitivist literary joke, it was much admired at the time for its picturesque layout and its successful visual combination of various cottage styles.

Loudon, who, not surprisingly, approved of his former draftsman's work, had also singled out the village of Harlaxton in Lincolnshire as a model for

The village of Edensor, Derbyshire, c.1830. Laid out by William Robertson to nestle in a valley out of sight of Chatsworth House, it is an elaborate concoction of mostly Italian-style houses.

Decimus Burton's design for a 'rustic village' at Furze Hill: a kaleidoscope of many of the styles of cottage architecture.

would-be Picturesque village-builders. It was not a new village but a remodelling of an existing model village of 'the plainest character' owned by Sir George de Ligne Gregory. It had been remodelled into a collection of Italian, French, Swiss and Old English cottages with decorative chimneytops, new porches, loggias, gables and hips, parapets and bargeboards. Each cottage garden was carefully planted out with creepers and climbing plants which were encouraged to wind their way up the cottage walls and over the fences and garden walls. Although Loudon waxed enthusiastic about it, Harlaxton's Picturesque qualities reside more in the arrangement of planting and the massing than in its appearance.

Butterfield's Baldersby of the mid century was in a sense vernacular revival building in the same way as his church was Gothic Revival. It was an attempt to create an air of authentic antiquity. And down in Kent, at Lord de Lisle's Penshurst Place, George Devey had already started to create the Old English village of Penshurst. It was, in fact, a mixture of remodelling and new building in the best materials and executed in the most skilful and expensive craftsmanship, so that today, apart from its mature and extensive planting, it looks much as it must have over a century ago. Then it looked very convincingly like a two- or three-century-old village which had been added to and altered in that casual, natural pattern of vernacular building. Blaise Hamlet had found a worthy successor. The Picturesque theorists would have been very satisfied with it – and, Price in particular, with Devey himself for he had acquired his knowledge and understanding of rural buildings and the rural scene as a student of the Norwich landscape artist John Sell Cotman and under J.D. Harding the topographical artist who had drawn the plates for several of the best Old English cottage-books in the 1830s. The Picturesque chain had been given another link.

Estate village building was to continue through the century and develop into a major activity – literally hundreds were built in England and later in Wales and Scotland. Many of them were of little Picturesque or even architectural interest.

When in the 1870s Jonathan Carr decided to build a suburban village, Bedford Park, at Turnham Green, London, the pattern of social life had changed. This village, built (rather roughly) to parsonage-style designs by E.W. Goodwin and tidied-up Old English designs by Norman Shaw, was aimed at the young artistic set, with a club, stores, inn, tennis courts and church where the new inhabitants could live out a suburbanized, culturalized version of the simple life – no aged retainers these sheltering under the benevolent shadow of the manor house up the road.

Bedford Park was Picturesque only by comparison with standard London terrace housing with its straight streets of uniform façades and little in the way of natural planting or gardens. But it was to provide an inspiration for the garden suburbs of the early twentieth century whose broad streets and vaguely Old English vernacular styling cast only a brief glance back at the compact and tightly integrated arrangement of Blaise. However much the vast population of the twentieth century demanded to regain touch with nature and the simple rural life, its sheer scale made it almost impossible to think any longer in the simple visual terms of the Picturesque. All that was left were a few decorative details.

CHAPTER SEVEN

Poverty, Politics and Philanthropy

Many of the Picturesque cottages built in England were real cottages for the peasantry. Built singly in the form of gate and estate lodges, in pairs (for economy and mutual comfort), in terraces and in hamlets, they were to be found all over the countryside. Often, as we have seen, their picturesqueness was a matter of attaching a few cheap vernacular details such as rustic branches around the porch, timber strapwork across the front façade in imitation of half timbering, as at Somerleyton, curly bargeboards as at Old Warden, and decorative thatching, as at Sandy, Bedfordshire.

Very often they were merely one or two rooms enclosed by a rustic veranda and topped with a simple thatched roof in a vague gesture towards the supposed original architectural model, the primitive hut. On occasion they were very elaborate, matching the architecture of the great house of the estate, or the philanthropic builder's notion of what a peasant village should look like.

By no means all model cottages and hamlets were designed by architects or were particularly Picturesque. Those that were, represented the icing on a relatively large cake of rather dull and basic model cottage building which in one form or another has continued in Britain to the present time – in the last sixty years in the form of council housing.

Why build cottages?

There have been a number of good reasons for building cottages for the poor. In 1919, when the British Government started building council housing in a serious way, it was motivated by deep concern about the possibility of social revolution. As recently released Cabinet papers show, the Lloyd George Government's 'Homes for Heroes' house-building campaign was the result of its real fear of a Bolshevik-style uprising. In that year King George V made clear his view about the social usefulness of building cottages for the poor (and for the returned soldiery from the First World War): 'If unrest is to be converted into contentment, the provision of good houses may provide one of the most potent agents in that conversion.'

Old English Domestic cottage at Fonthill Gifford, Wiltshire, probably a design by one of the Redleaf School.

A hundred years earlier, the British Government had been through this scenario just after Waterloo, and two decades before that, around the time of the French Revolution, it had been through a rehearsal.

Since the beginning of Britain's agrarian revolution there had been a pattern of local, sporadic and occasionally violent unrest. It took the form of food riots, rick-burning, sit-ins at disliked local squires' halls and the like. It had been seen largely as a nuisance in the stable economic period of the second half of the eighteenth century, when harvests had been good, but it came into sharp focus with the beginning of the French Revolution and the subsequent execution of Louis XVI in 1792 and Marie Antoinette in 1793. Ominously, 1792 was also the year of the worst popular agitation Britain had known for a very long time.

In 1795 there was a Europe-wide famine. In Britain food prices climbed and parish rates began to soar, doubling over the last decade of the eighteenth century and in some cases quadrupling. This was also partly a consequence of a rapid increase in population and of the Enclosure Acts of the previous thirty years, by which large numbers of cottagers had been totally dispossessed. Those who had not were rarely left with a sufficient amount of land to farm in a way which could support their basic needs. That meant that far more people were thrown onto parish relief than the system could comfortably tolerate. With landowners' pockets significantly affected by parish rates and with fear that the working population was in a state of potential ferment, it was not surprising that repressive class legislation soon followed – and with it hangings, transportation and the hulks, the Tolpuddle Martyrs, the Peterloo massacre, the last Peasants' Revolt and much more in between.

Cottages in the service of order

One approach to the intertwined problems of unrest and unacceptable levels of parish rates which gained credibility was to re-institute a self-sustaining economy for the peasantry – the largest single group among the lower classes of the time.

The basic ingredients of the idea were that landowners should provide peasant families with a cottage, a small plot of land and a domestic animal or two, all at a cheap rent. This, so the argument went, would at a stroke soften the evident misery of the rural poor, especially in the winter when there was little or no work on neighbouring farms. As a consequence there would be fewer peasants calling on the parish rates.

Providing a cottage and the possibility of a small measure of economic independence would, so it was argued, offer the hope of a stable future – plus a spin-off for the national weal. William Pocock argued: 'Being able to maintain their families without parochial aid, their sentiments of honour will be preserved, their natural independence of mind unbroken by indigence and inactivity.' This he said, would result in 'temperance, strength and health' among a peasantry thus 'better fitted for the defence of their country when called upon'. The war with Napoleon added another dimension to the parish rates and food prices problem – and the cottage plus land plus cow proposal offered something towards its solution as well.

At the same time, because the newly housed cottager had a vested interest in the good opinion of his landlord, he would be far less likely to go rioting. With the landowner in the role of honorary peasant paterfamilias, in the style of rural life of yore, the peasant would '… therefore consider that in promoting the interests of his landlord … he is at the same time promoting his own'. Or so argued Robert Beaston, a late eighteenth-century writer on the topic.

The bones of this idea were to be found in an Elizabethan law, recently repealed but long unobserved, which forbade the building of cottages with less than four acres of land attached. In the 1780s and 1790s it was developed as a social and economic argument by a number of agricultural observers and one or two architects, and in the late 1790s it emerged with semi-official approval in the pages of *Communications to the Board of Agriculture*, an annual government publication started in 1797 with the main function of spreading information about the agricultural state of the country, a kind of supplement to the county-by-county surveys which the Board had been carrying out for some time. Its first ten issues paid particular attention to the problems posed by the poverty of rural workers, and in 1801 and 1802 it actually offered prizes for the best schemes for reducing the parish rates. None seems to have been awarded.

Although it promoted the cottage plus land plus animal idea with enthusiasm, *Communications* was realistic about the real cost. Such schemes as it knew about had either been very carefully managed and occasionally broken even or ended up costing slightly more than paying increasing parish rates. The real benefits had to be found in the less tangible terms of a contented, non-rioting local peasantry.

The cottage homes of England

These arguments were all couched in economic or political terms but there were, of course, commentators who were genuinely shocked at the plight of the rural poor. Nathaniel Kent, a leading agricultural writer, introduced the first book on minimum cottage standards, *Hints to Landowners*, indignant at the '... shattered hovels which half the kingdom are obliged to put up with. It is truly affecting to a heart fraught with humanity ... neither health or decency can be preserved in them.' And the great architect of Bath, John Wood, put out a similar set of ideal plans for simple cottages soon after, in 1781, with a similar depth of feeling. Encouraged by a group of landowners to look at the state of local cottages, he came back from his survey horrified. He found them for the most part '... shattered, dirty, inconvenient, miserable hovels, scarcely affording a shelter for the beasts of the forest, much less were they the proper habitations for the human species'.

It also needs to be said that on large estates such as Nuneham Courtenay, Milton and Lowther there existed long-established traditions of housing local estate workers in cottages, and in the late eighteenth century there was a belief, not entirely unfounded, that the old-style landowner understood his responsibilities to his dependents as well as his privileges. But, as with all good-old-days mythologies, Milton and Lowther were exceptions to the rule,

Etching from real cottage life by James 'Antiquity' Smith in *Remarks on Rural Scenery* (1797) gives some idea of the realities of cottage life around the turn of the century – although Smith was at pains to point out that his concern was purely with visual matters.

and the average squire was in practice more insistent on his privileges than on his responsibilities – unless, as in the case of massively rising parish rates at the beginning of the nineteenth century, his pocket was also affected.

It is difficult today to envisage the squalor in which the average rural worker lived – or to understand the utter indifference of most of the middle and upper classes to the plight of the rural poor. The closest analogy today is the comfortably-off tourist travelling through the shanty towns of Third World countries. Like the modern tourist in those foreign countries, the indifferent eighteenth- and nineteenth-century landowner, parson and professional man drove through a countryside scattered with the tumbledown shacks of agricultural workers built from whatever was to hand: mud, turf, wattle and daub, and even road scrapings, with turf or thatch roofs and earth floors, and without sanitation. They were leaky, windy and often shared with domestic animals.

The average size of a rural worker's cottage at the end of the eighteenth century was one room with perhaps a sleeping loft, occupied by sometimes seven or eight people. This is not imaginative extrapolation from one or two records or anecdotes, such as those of Kent and Wood, but is based on data to be found in the official *County Reports* published by the Board of Agriculture in the 1790s. Only the most soundly built peasant dwellings have survived to this day to perpetuate the mythology of cosy cottage life and to join the queue for late twentieth-century gentrification. The rest fell apart quite soon.

The cottage homes of Britain were often built under the ancient squatting rights of common law which countenanced the existence of a dwelling if it had been put up and occupied without detection. That, tradition had it, meant starting building work at sunset and having a fire going in the 'hearth' by the following sunrise. Even if most cottages were not built under this rule, they looked and performed as though they had been.

As to class attitudes to the peasantry, it needs to be stressed to modern generations brought up on the mythology of the yeomen of England that the word 'peasant' was in universal currency in the eighteenth century as a description for the rural worker, and long into the Victorian period. It did not describe quite the same economic and social state as that of his European counterpart – the difference being between agricultural wage labourer and European direct family cultivator, but 'peasant' was the word used and it was used by middle and upper classes to describe people who were members of almost another race. The word 'race' also occurs commonly in contemporary literature about the peasantry, and it was used by even the most sympathetic of writers. Nathaniel Kent, friend of the cottager, talked about the species thus: 'Cottagers are indisputably the most beneficial race of people we have: they are bred up in great simplicity; live more primitive lives, more free from vice and debauchery than any other set of men of the lower class.'

The step from this position to the idealization of the cottager as a species of Noble Savage was but a short one. It was a useful one too, for it enabled contemporary Englishmen to take a detached view of what they saw around them, in the manner of the modern tourist in the shanty towns of South America. William Gilpin, a kindly New Forest parson, has a typical passage in his famous *Observations on the River Wye*, the book which made his reputation as a major aesthetician and started the fashion for touring the British countryside and observing its picturesque beauties. Journeying down the Wye his party comes to Tintern Abbey – romantically aweful, venerable and picturesque. He enthuses about the scene, but notes one or two unexpected curiosities: 'In this scene of desolation, the poverty and wretchedness of the inhabitants were remarkable. They occupy little huts, raised among the ruins of the monastery; and seem to have no employment but begging.' The party comes upon one of these huts: 'We did not expect to be interested: but we found we were. I never saw so loathesome a human dwelling ... we were rather [more] surprised that the wretched inhabitant was still alive; than that she had only lost the use of her limbs.' Oblivious of the casual callousness about this 'interesting' experience, the gentle parson-aesthete and his party moved on down the river in search of more visual delight in the hanging woods and steep sides and rushing water of their picturesque tour.

It is the same kind of detachment which enabled the artist James 'Antiquity' Smith a decade or two later to make his reputation and living from sketching and engraving views of picturesque grinding poverty in the form of picturesque beggars and picturesque cottages. He was indeed slightly ashamed of this but advanced the standard Romantic defence of Art transcending Life in explanation.

But we should not be too censorious of individuals in a society whose hymnals contained verses about squires in their castles, peasants at their gates and all remaining in their proper places; a society which accepted the traditional lot of the lower orders and which at the level of sophisticated Malthusian economic theory saw the elements of want and misery as integral parts of the process which regulated the balance between domestic food production and increases in population in Britain's still primarily agricultural economy. Both the immutable social order of things and high economic doctrine demanded an acceptance by the peasant of his lot – and of his appalling housing.

Although the suggested minimum standards which John Wood had outlined in 1781 in his *A Series of Plans for Cottages or Habitations for the Labourer* were greatly to influence thinking about cottage design in the semi-government publication *Communications to the Board of Agriculture* and were to become the standard for the best kind of model cottage building for a century to follow, they were only marginally effective on the lot of the mass of agricultural workers. In 1839, to take a date at random, the annual mortality rate from fever alone among the rural poor (double the death toll at Waterloo) was admitted in the House of Lords to be the result of the

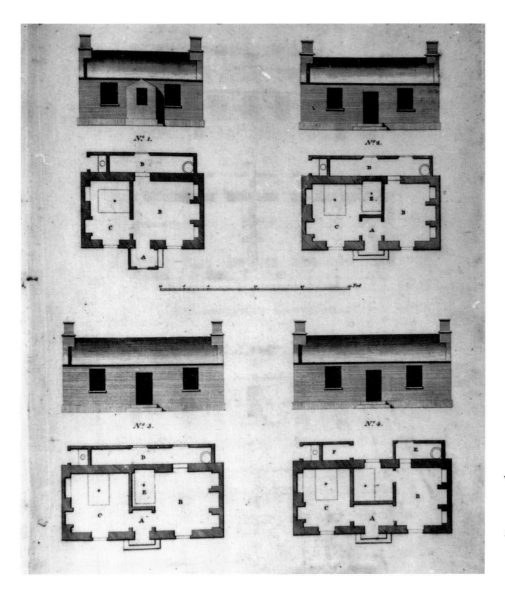

Model peasant cottage designs by John Wood, 1781. Unusually there is space for storage, washing and privies – the fact that these represented a desirable standard gives some indication of the lot of the average cottager of the time.

appalling conditions in which agricultural workers still lived. Even in Edwardian times the evidence, both documentary and, by then, photographic, indicates that neither wages nor living conditions had much changed since the eighteenth century. Then, as in the eighteenth century, the crucial regulator of living and housing conditions was whether the peasant earned enough to keep himself at or above the subsistence level and not whether benevolent and philanthropic people agitated for the betterment of his housing condition.

Many cottages and model village were of the most utilitarian kind, but in a country which had developed the aesthetic theory of the Picturesque, which was under the general sway of Romantic thinking and which had in the wings a small crowd of architects anxious to make their way, it is not surprising that an equal number were decorated in the voguish Picturesque manner.

Many of the young architects were thoroughly familiar with the literature about minimum cottage standards and the cottage plus land plus cow panacea to be found in Wood and the Board of Agriculture's *Communications*, and they were not backward in supporting and promoting them for here was ready-made semi-official endorsement for cottage architecture. But architects naturally wanted to promote their own services as well. Joseph Gandy, a young architect in 1805, set out the would-be cottage architect's position by noting approvingly the existence of ideal plans published in *Communications* and elsewhere. Entirely virtuous and helpful they were, he pointed out, yet they '... relate chiefly to the modes of construction ... and other local particulars: objects unquestionably of the first importance and which should never be lost sight of. But the advancement of Public Taste requires more than this – that we should combine convenience of arrangement with elegance in the external appearance.'

For Gandy, this appeal for the advancement of public taste fell on deaf ears. His forte turned out to be architectural illustration. But for many other architects, promoting the idea of combining decent accommodation for the peasantry with a decorative outer coat turned out to be the way to success.

One reason for this was the currency of the idea, already noted, that building cottages which, however vaguely, looked like vernacular peasant dwellings would result in their peasant occupants acting out the roles of happy peasants in real life. It is reputed that in the late eighteenth century the Prince de Ligne's peasants at Belœil had literally to do so. They were obliged to dress up in peasant rags and, when a bell rang to announce strollers through the garden, spring into action, milking cows, singing on the green and carrying out bucolic activities – a kind of theatrical performance to go with the carefully designed rural landscape setting. So too in England, in satirical writing at least, it is said that some landowners hired hermits by the week to inhabit the rustic 'hermitages' dotting their Picturesque landscaped gardens – although there is no good evidence that this occurred in reality.

That kind of thing would, of course, never do with the sturdy British peasantry, which was not, as its European counterpart was, in a feudal relationship with the local lord. There were those, however, who could fantasize. William Mason, the landscape poet, for example, suggested

Rustic/vernacular picturesque cottage in the paternalistic village of Old Warden, Bedfordshire.

employing strings of peasant girls dressed up as milkmaids as a living substitute for ugly fences in the fields. To their credit, his contemporaries found this idea ludicrously funny. There is an apocryphal story that in the mid-nineteenth century the peasant tenants of the cottages in the thatch and curly bargeboard Bedfordshire village of Old Warden had to wear red cloaks and pointed hats as they went about their business in the village street in something of the Belœil fashion – and of modern folklore museums.

If the economic independence of the British peasant (compared, that is with his European counterpart) precluded his regular casting in living landscape theatre roles, there was a role for him on the philanthropic stage. For the early nineteenth-century picturesque cottager, there, up at the big house, dwelled Lady Bountiful.

There are passages in Cobbett's famous *Rural Rides* through the English countryside in the early nineteenth century which outline the kinds of conditions which Picturesque cottage builders demanded from their newly housed peasants, such as regular attendance at church. And the day-to-day social control is nauseatingly and smugly outlined by one of the best designers of Picturesque cottages, P.F. Robinson: 'A morning is frequently dedicated to visit the thriving family [which has been given a P.F. Robinson cottage in which to live]. The attention of the landlord is met by the assiduity of the tenant and neatness and even elegance is the result.... The good wife, anxious to please her benefactress and grateful for the attention paid to her, is ever on the watch for the morning visit and is consequently always in order.' Still, the horrors of the workhouse were greater, and what fragmentary evidence remains suggests that the lives of villagers in Picturesque developments were frequently regulated either by written rules of behaviour or by this kind of moral suasion.

In real life, Picturesque peasant Arcadia was brought about rather than developing, Rousseau-fashion, by simple men going about their simple lives and learning from the great Teacher Nature. It needs to be added that, at a less close-grained scale than this, the relationship between country landlord and village tenant had remained unchanged to the present day – according to tenants in some parts of Britain.

CHAPTER EIGHT

The Domestic Revival

Few architects in Britain published books of Picturesque cottage designs after around the middle of the nineteenth century. In the US the tradition was carried over by such writers as A.J. Downing, Calvert Vaux and Gervase Wheeler, who turned the principles of the Picturesque cottage in a uniquely American direction. But that did not mean the end of Picturesque cottage building in Britain or in any way the end of the Picturesque as the underlying philosophy of generations of architects to come.

On the one hand it was the central theme of the later nineteenth-century wave of English Arts and Crafts domestic architecture culminating in the Domestic Revival – and the USA's contemporary Stick and Shingle styles. Also it has recently been reworked in the late twentieth century, in only slightly updated form, by British architects preoccupied with the moral virtues of the Neo-vernacular style for housing. And over the whole period in between, in various disguises and simplified forms, the descendants of the picturesque cottage have been built in a thousand housing developments around the Anglo-Saxon world.

Although the cottage books were no longer being published, builders continued to work from them more or less directly. Rustic, gothic, Italian, vernacular, Old English and cottage ornée cottages were built right through into the twentieth century. The guest wing at Hever Castle, built around 1904 for Lord Astor by the architect F.L. Pearson, took the form of an Old English village which could have been designed by P.F. Robinson – although it was sixty years after his death. Rustic cottages continued to be built at the edge of great estates for decades.

Through the rest of the nineteenth century and into the twentieth, when philanthropists, utopians or landowners decided to build model villages and hamlets, there was a good chance that they would continue to choose a vaguely vernacular or Old English style. Sometimes it was done in a quite sophisticated way; more commonly it was a matter of sticking picturesquely styled detailing onto rather mundane brick boxes.

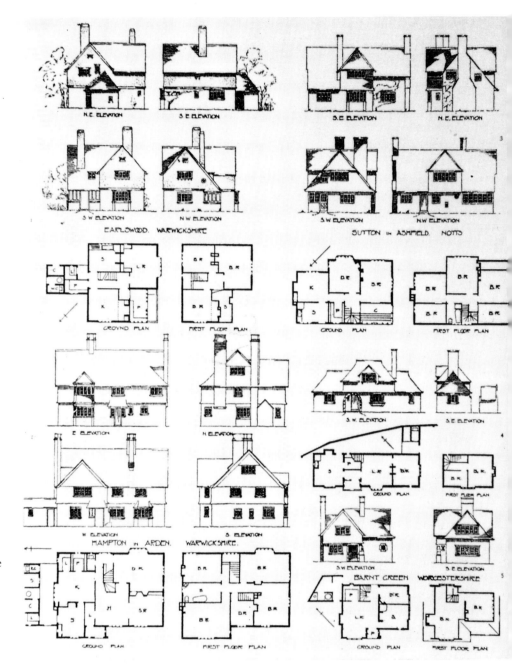

A miscellany of cottage and house designs by Bateman and Bateman of around 1900. There is not much to chose between these and the designs of, say, Malton a hundred years before – right down to the irregular plans and choice of variegated materials for walls and roofs.

The nineteenth-century philanthropic housing and village tradition was to develop into the larger-scale urban housing estate movements of the early part of the twentieth century – forerunners of massive state involvement in British public housing from the 1920s until the present time.

During the interwar years a crude, simplified mixture of Old English and vernacular decoration became standard for many of the new British public housings schemes. A similar sketchy version of Old English decoration was widely used by inter-war speculative housing developers who were sprawling their suburbs outwards from the centres of British cities. It became jokingly known to sophisticates as Tudorbethan or Tudoresque and, in the wealthier Home counties, Stockbroker Tudor.

The Domestic Revival

Builders and the occasional architect continued to build cottages in the styles of the 1830s and 40s, but the Picturesque was a living, dynamic force and the most imaginative developments of the Picturesque cottage tradition were centred on the vernacular and the old English styles. In practice the Old English was simply a more 'architecturalized' version of the vernacular style. Both styles were based on the indigenous, local architecture of England, and the two stemmed directly from the same central Picturesque preoccupation with Nature.

When the 1890s versions of Old English and vernacular had been 'discovered' by Herman Muthesius and admiringly chronicled in his 1904 *Das Englische Haus*, which was immediately and widely read by the early European Arts and Crafts architects and designers, they acquired the rather inaccurate omnibus description 'New Free Style' – or, as later historians would have it, the English Domestic Revival. It was, in fact, not a brand-new architectural movement or a revival, simply a gradual evolution and sophistication of fundamental Picturesque thinking and Picturesque visual preferences.

What had happened was that by the middle of the century architects had finally got over much of their excitement at being able to design in any way they chose. They had begun to look for solid precedents for their design among the traditions of native culture, among the hills, dales, villages and hamlets of their own countryside. These were the very subjects of the new landscape painting pioneered by Constable and the Norwich School, developed and continued by the nineteenth-century English landscape school and supported by the parallel school of writing and poetry which celebrated the unique qualities of the English countryside. And the young architects of the 1860s and later such as Eden Nesfield and Norman Shaw, began to go

Large cottage near Penshurst in the Old English Domestic style: completely confident composition and handling of vernacular materials.

into the countryside armed with sketching pads and pencils in search of the 'true' British architectural heritage.

These two were members of a loose group of painters and architects based in Kent and Surrey, a number of them associated with the collector and patron William Wells who lived at Redleaf, Penshurst. He was to commission George Devey, a generation older than Shaw and Nesfield, to design an Old English vernacular cottage for him, a successor to an attempt he had himself made at vernacular design in the late 1820s. Within a couple of decades, under the influence of Wells and other like-minded patrons and artists, the surrounding villages in Surrey and Kent were populated with vernacular cottages designed by young architects fired with a desire to re-create the spirit of the simple rural tradition of their country. Not a few of their clients were landscape artists.

Sketching tours in the country, 'scrambles' as they were known, soon became an essential feature of the lives of young architects. They gave the pleasure of rambling a high moral purposefulness. They were sanctioned by the contemporary habit of landscape artists who went on sketching tours as a matter of course, and they were a serious-minded substitute for the Continental architectural sketching tours which only the wealthier of them could afford. It is notable that, as had been the case with Barry and P.F. Robinson, the notebooks of those architects who could afford such a tour were filled with views of the vernacular scenery and buildings of Italy, France and Germany quite as much as with the architectural antiquities of the classical past.

The cumulative effect of these scrambles was to build up a very considerable body of first-hand knowledge of traditional British buildings and of their details and construction. And often a scramble provided the opportunity to sketch the detailing and forms of the latest architect-designed Old English houses and cottages as well – a neat case of art imitating art imitating nature. This was an important way of keeping architects abreast of each other's work and of providing cribs and details for young architects grappling with the difficult problems of Picturesque vernacular detail design. One spin-off was a tremendous surge of book publishing on the topic of native traditional building which was not to die out until the 1920s.

Equally important, the experience of seeing the countryside at first hand and collecting information about it provided excellent background for architects who were to join the various Arts and Crafts societies which started up in the 1880s under the influence of the back-to-nature, anti-machine writing and lecturing of William Morris. His call was for an architecture based on traditional vernacular sources, for hand-crafting and

Charles Rennie Macintosh's design for Hill House, Helensburgh, 1902. Irregular vernacular forms and traditional materials.

NORTH ELEVATION

GROUND FLOOR PLAN

Edwin Lutyens'
house in Devonshire
in local stone with
grey tiles, c.1906.

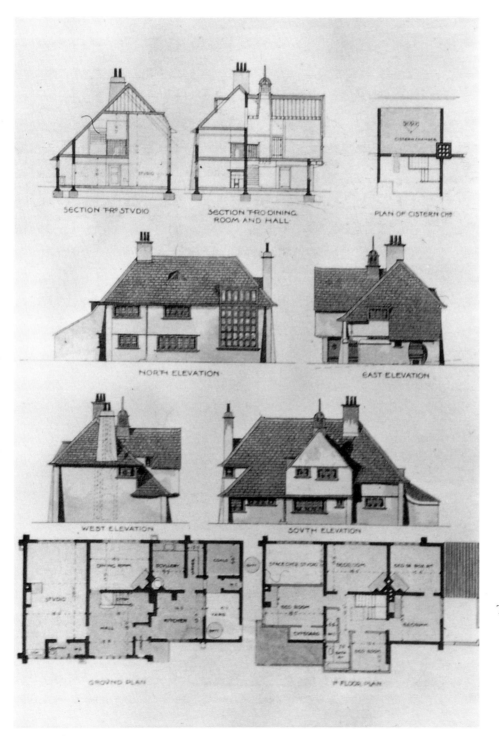

SECTION TR° STUDIO

SECTION TR° DINING.
ROOM AND HALL·

PLAN OF CISTERN CH°

NORTH ELEVATION·

EAST ELEVATION

WEST ELEVATION

SOUTH ELEVATION

GROUND PLAN

1° FLOOR PLAN

Typical Voysey house with green rain barrels, green slates, rough cast brick and asymmetrical form and plan. Designed for Alfred Sutro, artist, at Studland Bay, Dorset.

for consonance in architecture with Nature. He said, 'It is from necessary [functional], unpretentious buildings that the new style and genuine architecture will spring rather than from our experiments in conscious style.'

Since all that had been implicitly accepted by the inheritors of the Picturesque architectural tradition, it is not surprising that Morris was widely popular among architects. For young architects who had probably not read the writings of Knight, Price and Repton of eighty years before, it was a clarion call – especially when their elders, in whose offices they had trained, had, as their practices acquired grander and grander commissions, moved away from vernacular in the direction of quasi-classical styles.

Among these young architects were Guy Dawber, Robert Weir Schulz, Edward Prior, Ernest Gimson, Halsey Ricardo, Edwin Lutyens, Walter Cave, Detmar Blow, C.F.A. Voysey and, in Scotland, Charles Rennie Mackintosh. Their buildings abandoned much of the directly imitative vernacular and Old English detailing of their seniors – it was 'traditional' or vernacular in spirit rather than in form, although Ernest Gimson's Stonywell Cottage at Markfield in Leicestershire has much of the feeling of an early cottage ornée or vernacular-style building in its irregular arrangement of rooms, roofs, dormers and jettying wrapped around a vast spreading chimney. Inside, the vernacular theme is taken to an extreme, for one of the bedrooms could be reached only by ladder.

Of this group Edwin Schroeder Prior was probably the most determinedly individualist, building quite large houses in a rambling cottage style, experimenting with novel ways of enlivening wall surfaces and using, not always with great success, new patented building materials.

The group's leading figure was C.F.A. Voysey. This was a matter partly of sheer inventive talent and partly of his nose for publicity: almost all his pre-war cottages and houses were published in the architectural magazines, and his practice flourished. After the Great War, when his fellow neo-vernacularists almost to a man changed stylistic horses in the direction of classicism, Voysey remained consistent to the declining end of his days, using the same approach to grand houses and cottages – large enveloping roofs, small windows, spreading, sensible plans, rough stuccoed walls, tall central chimneys, often serving a cluster of hearths inside, ramping buttresses outside. His design was vernacular in spirit and feeling rather than a direct imitation of vernacular forms – still Picturesque in its aesthetic sense and as carefully composed visual treats. As Herman Muthesius, the German chronicler of the Domestic Revival, said of his approach to design: 'The way he does this is always in the simplest and most direct fashion, so that his houses always hint at vernacular and unsophisticated origins.'

Opposite: A design for a double cottage by A.N. Prentice.

DESIGN FOR A PAIR
OF COTTAGES

FRONT ELEVATION.

SIDE ELEVATION.

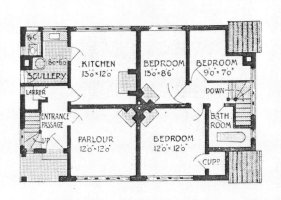

GROUND PLAN   FIRST FLOOR PLAN

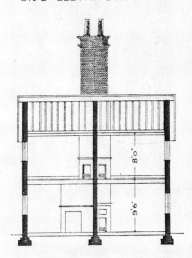

SECTION A.A.

SCALE   FEET

MATERIALS: CUMBERLAND SLATES, RED BRICK AND ROUGHCAST, WOOD WINDOW FRAMES PAINTED GREEN

Voysey himself maintained that the architect should return to Nature for his source of inspiration, that, following the old vernacular traditions, he should use his materials in an honest and direct fashion. Here of course was the basic Picturesque position, with strong overtones of the Utilitarian argument about beauty as a direct function of the fitness of purpose of the design or object. Said Voysey, 'Try the effect of a well-proportioned room, with whitewashed walls, plain carpet and simple oak furniture and nothing in it but necessary articles of use – and one pure ornament in the form of a simple vase of flowers ... '

That was Voysey's official austere position but his work had what his critics described as a curious *Alice in Wonderland* atmosphere: Hansel and Gretel windows, heart motifs painted on shutters, doors and the large green water butts which he regularly introduced in his design drawings, together with the addition of an occasional gothic element – a fairytale touch of chocolate-box Picturesqueness, an echo of the nuttier cottage ornée designs of the early part of the century. But it would be un-Picturesque not to allow eccentricities in the leading inheritor of that tradition.

Yet what, more importantly, he and his young contemporaries were doing was taking the naturalized vernacular architecture of their countryside and 'with new thought and feeling', to use Voysey's own words, create a new domestic architecture. Predicated as it was on a belief in the naturalness and rightness of vernacular building, it was not, of course, all that new.

In one collection of these new house and cottage designs the architect William Bidlake began in a fashion uncannily reminiscent of James Malton in 1798 with several pages in praise of the real vernacular cottage and several more against the hard-edged brick stereotype houses of late eighteenth-century classicism. Introducing his fellow vernacularists, Bidlake emphasized that their designs were '... not copies ... Here the traditional has been selected only as a basis to work upon: its elements have been modified and recombined, they are adapted to meet the needs of the present day. We do not want a new style. We are reverend as a people and we are not only proud of the heritage which our fathers have left us but we wish to feel that our dwelling houses trace their lineage alike from those of old times and echo by their similar disposition of stone gable or mullioned window some of the romance that attaches to old buildings.' Here is the nostalgia, nationalsim and a dose of country common sense of a century before.

In the best early nineteenth century cottage-book tradition these were 'adapted to the needs of the present day'. The 'needs' had changed a little over the century: within their steep-pitched roofs, leaded windows, irregular forms and folksy air often lurked bathrooms, internal lavatories and, in the case of one Lutyens design, bicycle cupboards by the front door.

The USA

British architects had the continuity of the Picturesque domestic tradition but a no less vigorous and no less Picturesque approach to cottage and house design began to develop in the USA in the late 1830s. It was to develop along parallel lines to the Arts and Crafts and Domestic Revival architecture of contemporary Britain in the form of what has now come to be called the Stick and Shingle styles. It looked for its inspiration in two directions – back at traditional American building and across the Atlantic to Britain's Picturesque domestic design. That connection was to continue through the rest of the century and, as in Britain, architectural publications were the main means of spreading and popularizing the new attitudes.

Among the earliest Picturesque cottage-books published in the USA were those of A.J. Davis (*Rural Residences*, 1837) and A.J. Downing, who had visited Britain in the 1830s and had met the architectural and landscape encyclopaedist John Claudius Loudon. On his return he brought out *Cottage Residences* and *The Architecture of Country Houses* in 1850. Calvert Vaux, who had followed Downing back to the USA, brought out his *Villas and Cottages* in 1857.

These books of Picturesque cottage and house designs follow the pattern and the fundamental Picturesque message of earlier British cottage books. For example, in his 1850 *The Architecture of Country Houses*, Downing thus describes an 'English-style' gate lodge (which is reminiscent of designs by Lugar, Nash and Pocock of the first decade of the nineteenth century): 'The chief merits of this cottage is its picturesqueness.... Placed among fine groups of trees, with a well wooded background, this design would have a striking and most agreeable effect because the variety and irregularity of its outline would be supported by the varied forms of foliage and bough.' The principles of the Pictureque applied to the relationship between buildings and setting whatever the location. It was not accidental that Downing and Vaux were also the earliest major landscape designers of the new world, Vaux later forming a partnership with the great Frederick Law Ohlmsted whose development of Picturesque landscape design transformed vast tracts of the American landscape.

Although many of the designs in these books would have been familiar to a British reader, the general tenor of their authors was in the direction of creating a recognizably American domestic architecture. One obviously American feature was a preference for traditional American timber construction with vertical siding rather than the brick nogging, weatherboarding or brick preferred (and more readily available) in Britain. It was also partly to do with form. Downing, for example, contrasts one of his

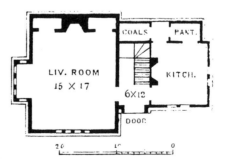

Design for a small
bracketed cottage by
A.J. Downing in *The
Architecture of
Country Houses*:
local timber-cladding
tradition.

designs for an American farmhouse with a similar design in the 'English Rural' style: 'There is, perhaps, in this house, a little more independence and a little less lowliness manifested, both being expressed in the higher stories, and the greater space from the ground to the eaves in this design.' American farmers, thought Downing, would prefer it, not only because the warmer American climate made higher ceilings more practical but '…mainly because American farmers love independence above all things, and hence instinctively and unconsciously lay hold of anything that manifests it'.

There was also a consonance between the Picturesque and American independence and vigour. 'As force of expression should rightly spring from force of character, so Picturesque Architecture, where its picturesqueness grows out of strong character in the inhabitant, is the more interesting to most minds.' Price Knight and Repton in their ordered society of half a century before could hardly have anticipated this extension of their aesthetic argument.

Downing, Vaux and other American cottage-book authors devoted considerable space to examining local materials, climate, living habits and building practices. These, together with a growing self-esteem and an increasing interest in American Colonial architecture, were to be the important elements in modifying the British approach.

Although house designs by H.H. Richardson, Charles McKim and Richard Morris Hunt of the 1870s and later were much influenced by designs published in the British architectural magazines, the flavour soon became unmistakably American – drawing as it did as much on wood-frame American vernacular and rural building traditions as on the Arts and Crafts architects interpretation of their own country's vernacular.

Towards the end of the century, as American architects became more interested in looking to continental Europe rather than to Britain, the Californian architects Green and Green brought the vernacular tradition to a highly sophisticated height: rough wood, shingles, cobblestones, spreading verandas and internal planning of remarkable freedom which was to inspire (as had the British Arts and Crafts architects) a great wave of suburban bungalow building in a similar, vaguely vernacular style and the uniquely American and rather craftsy Woodbutcher's houses of the West Coast.

This was tradition which underlay the form and the philosophy of the great American Frank Lloyd Wright's architecture: his spreading roofs, central hearths, sprawling plans, nature-based ornament and belief in an 'organic architecture' were brilliantly conceived extensions of the Picturesque vernacular domestic tradition – in his hands quite transformed in time and place and conception from the simple labourers' cottages of James Malton a century before.

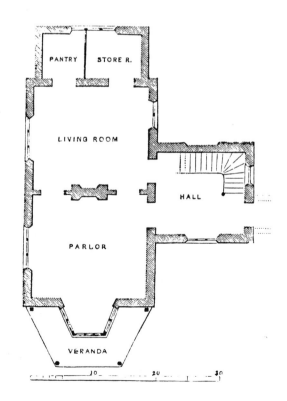

A gate lodge in the
English style. One of
many Picturesque
cottage designs for
the USA in A.J.
Downing's book *The
Architecture of
Country Houses*
(1850).

Twenties and thirties

When, around the time of the First World War, the California Mission style overtook the Stick and Shingle style vernacular on the West Coast, it was, in a sense, merely a case of one vernacular style replacing another in popular building. Arguably it was one which was visually more indigenous to the locality than the timber-frame tradition of the East and Mid West, although it was constructed in stuccoed timber framing. One architect, however, Bernard Maybeck, continued doggedly in the vernacular tradition – in much the same fashion as C.F.A. Voysey – long after it had ceased to be fashionable. In a series of remarkable houses around the Berkeley University campus in timber, shingle and occasionally stone, with loggias, verandas, open plans, wide eaves and exposed rafters, Maybeck continued an American combination of simplicity and naturalism with an underlying high Arts and Crafts purpose of creating a better moral and aesthetic life for his fellows.

In Britain, after the post-war loss of architectural nerve, the Picturesque vernacular cottage tradition was to shift uneasily into the realm of mass housing and speculative development. It became one of the stylistic options for designers of the early garden suburbs and any amount of British public housing in the 1920s and 1930s. Vestigial Picturesque detailing in the form of vaguely Old English strapwork and stucco, together with dormers and simplified curly bargeboards, bow windows and steep little roofs, were about all that remained.

Yet in one or two cases, such as that of the architect-developer Ernest Trobridge, some of the more amusing aspects of the Picturesque were revived. In the London suburb of Kingsbury he built a series of houses and developments in a curious mixture of cottage ornée and castellated gothic styles the like of which had not been seen since the early, wild period around 1800. Most the these semi-vernacular houses were built in timber, and they were very cheap at the time: Trobridge's search for economies neatly tied in the pattern of the vernacular builder seeking to go about his craft in the most direct fashion. He preferred thatch, on the grounds that it was lighter and required less structural support and low ceiling because they called for less walling outside. As he himself is reported to have said, he had adopted the olde worlde style not 'as an antiquarian enthusiast but as a practical architect'. Unexpectedly, beneath the thatch and timberwork is to be found a prefabricated structural timber framework patented by Trobridge. It can be no accident that he was a fervent disciple of Emanuel Swedenborg, the eighteenth-century nature-philosopher.

1930s thatched
cottage by Ernest
Trobridge at
Kingsbury, London.

CHAPTER NINE

Stockbroker Tudor and the Modern Age

In an overwhelmingly urban post-war society it is probably not very surprising that the dream of a cottage in the country has tightened its grip on the Anglo-Saxon imagination, but the notion of actually building Picturesque cottages surely has no place in the modern world.

In the 1970s and 80s, in fact, quite the contrary has been the case, for in Britain something close to the forms and thinking of the early nineteenth century has resurfaced. Lord and Lady Bountiful are now the architects, planners and housing committees of local authorities, the style is called Neo-vernacular, and the call is the return to the old dream of a comfortable, homely cottage with a garden and a front porch, tiled roofs, brick walls, tile hanging, dormer windows and climbing plants, designed in casual, irregular formations on quiet village streets.

It has been, on the one hand, a sharp reaction from the regimented, mechanistic rows and towers of grey concrete which were the *de rigueur* way to design public housing for nearly four decades, but it has also been a transliteration of the cottage-in-the-country dream into a kind of reality whose close parallels with the Primitivist attitudes of the late eighteenth century are all the more amusing because the protagonists are in most cases unaware that they belong not, as they believe, to some kind of fundamental cultural tradition but to the fashionable and often bizarre architectural tradition which this book has chronicled.

In the new-broom atmosphere after the end of the Second World War, housing became a grimly serious affair. In those reconstruction times the emphasis was on efficiency, and the somewhat fanciful pleasures of the Picturesque had no place. In Europe, housing was built or funded predominantly by the state and designed by young architects fired by the new style of the Modern Movement – an architecture of right-angles, precision and unsentimental clarity. In the US and Australia, whose major cities had not been partly destroyed by war, tract housing development took a different turn – homely, far more spread out on the ground and (except in central metropolitan zones) rarely in the economical form of the apartment blocks which were more or less the norm in Europe.

In Britain, some provincial local authorities still built paired cottages coated in roughcast stucco in the pre-war fashion but for a number of years after the war large local authorities faced with massive reconstruction work found building materials so scarce that the new sparse International Style was often a matter of economic necessity as much as aesthetic preference. By the 1970s, however, there had occurred a reaction to the soullessness of massive public housing redevelopment – especially in Britain. Even in the USA, where there was very little in the way of public housing, there was a dramatic reaction, and one infamous scheme, the Pruitt Igo development in Chicago, was blown up after it had become uninhabitable. Not to be outdone, in the early 1980s British housing authorities began to follow suit, and Sunday afternoon crowds regularly gathered to watch relatively new tower blocks being demolished by controlled explosion.

Tower blocks could hardly have been more antithetical to the cottage-in-the-country ideal, and the blowing up of a small selection of the worst of them was a metaphorical exclamation mark marking the end of one dead end and the return of the ideal to a central position in the thinking and imagery of architects and their clients.

Latter-day Lady Bountifuls, now in the guise of British housing authority committees, urged on by populist newspaper commentators and the occasional architectural writer, did their political and building cost sums and set themselves firmly on the side of a small-scale Picturesque approach to housing design. It was not called Picturesque, of course, and it was 'housing' rather than houses or cottages, but the general scenario would have been understood by any early nineteenth-century Picturesque cottage-builder.

Curiously, the seeds of this renewed interest in the cottage theme in housing were to be found the post-war work of that arch-Modernist and godfather of the tower blocks the French architect le Corbusier.

Formerly one of the most rigorous of rectilinear-form, strip-window and plain-concrete-wall architects, after the Second World War le Corbusier began to incorporate free forms into his buildings. He and his wide circle of admirers pointed out that this new approach owed a great deal to Mediterranean vernacular building. Soon the blocky pattern of cliffside and hillside villages constructed from whitewashed stone and clay began to take on an alluring abstract quality for British architects of the 1950s and 60s. Armed with cameras and slide film instead of the sketching pads and pencils of their fellow-countrymen 150 years before, they toured the hinterland and littoral towns of Italy and the Mediterranean in search less of the remains of the great architecture of the Italian Renaissance than, like their architectural predecessors, of that unselfconscious architecture which seemed to have grown from the landscape in which it was set. P.F. Robinson and Charles

Parker in the 1820s went in search of individual vernacular buildings but they would have understood their professional descendants' preoccupation with a search for irregular, rugged and intricate forms to record and take back to Britain, there to translate them into buildings for everyday people.

Here was an architecture which spoke directly to its viewers. It conformed to the Utilitarian idea of beauty coming about as the consequence of a direct response to local circumstances. It clearly represented a response to the local building resources and was seemingly formed and organized in response to the age-old social organization of small village settlements. It was, so the argument then went, an architecture without architects.

A whole new Primitivist scenario had been discovered (or rediscovered), a purpose-made model for the twentieth century's new problem of housing very large numbers of people – rather than, as had been the case in the 1800s, a group of estate workers. The essential difference was, however, merely a matter of scale.

Architecture Without Architects was the name of a very influential book published in the mid 1960s by architect Bernard Rudofsky. It was not much more than a collection of photographs of vernacular settlements, mainly from the Mediterranean region – the kind of photographs which thousands of architectural tourists had been taking for at least a decade. But its brief text, the quality of the photographs and the fact that it squared precisely with the back-to-basics elements which underlay Modern Movement architecture made it an immediate best seller.

Vernacular architecture seemed to solve the problem of eliminating impure elements in architecture such as style and decoration – and the moral wrongness of decoration and ornament and anything which was not essential was a major preoccupation of the Modern Movement.

As Rudofsky put it in his introduction, 'Vernacular architecture does not go through fashion cycles. It is nearly immutable, indeed unimprovable, since it serves its purpose to perfection....' The distant 1796 voice of James Malton introducing *British Cottage Architecture* is audible here.

Rudofsky's book had a number of spin-offs. One was to reinforce architects' interest in the use of off-the-form concrete, the modern version of those whitewashed stone and clay walls. Another was to encourage the design of housing schemes which spilled down hillsides or which were built up into artificial hillside settlements in the form of what were called megastructures. A small number of these were built, notably Moishe Safde's Habitat at the Montreal Expo, and several housing schemes in Britain – all of which, if you half closed your eyes, could have been lifted complete from some Mediterranean site and set down in the non-Mediterranean climates of Britain and Canada.

By the time these anglicized hillside villages were finally constructed, in the late 1960s and early 1970s, this approach to housing had lost favour. In any case, vernacular themes closer to home had been available for some time – and in the modern architectural writing and design of the great American architect Frank Lloyd Wright. Wright's call for an 'organic' architecture seemed to make sense in these relatively New World, recently frontier territories. There exigent nature was still often rawly in evidence in real life, and there too existed a certain amount of cultural pressure to develop an indigenous national architecture. What better approach could be followed than to draw deliberately on the visual and physical resources of local nature – which is to say, the local vernacular? For a time the old early nineteenth-century architectural warfare between the architecture of nature and the architecture of intellect and order resurfaced as modern designers aligned themselves behind either the Wrightian or the International Style banners. In practice the battle was confined largely to housing design.

During the 1950 and 1960s modern architects of the 'organic' vernacular school around the world, but notably in Australia and California, built a number of outstanding small houses designed in the locally plentiful timber

Photo from Rudofsky's evocative *Architecture without Architects* of a Moroccan fortified town (*Academy Editions*).

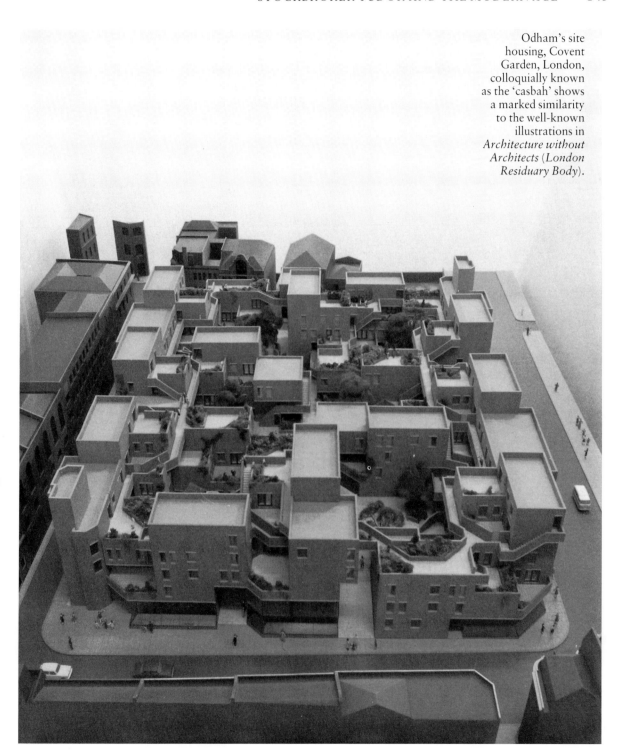

Odham's site housing, Covent Garden, London, colloquially known as the 'casbah' shows a marked similarity to the well-known illustrations in *Architecture without Architects* (*London Residuary Body*).

and brick and clapboard and occasionally galvanized iron (which had become a traditional building material in Australia). Occasionally there were to be found houses constructed from adobe and pise. These houses were designed in a way which emphasized the texture and structural nature of the materials and which were organized in a way which was at once casual and highly sophisticated. With the exception of examples in the US, where there had been a Spanish adobe construction tradition for a number of centuries, none of these areas could be said to have an extant vernacular tradition.

In Britain, where there was, a few architects, such as Stout and Litchfield, Aldington and Craig, experimented with the 'organic' approach, though without the spreading eaves and extensive rambling plans possible in the extensive building plots of the New World. For British vernacular architects it was brick, slate and clipped eaves – in some ways an apt parallel with the difficulty the British had in finding land, building materials and permission to build private houses which were not of the prevailing architectural fashion.

One of the most important early examples of such buildings was the Sugden House, at Watford by the then-famous architects Peter and Alison Smithson. Designed in the early 1950s, at a time of very scarce building resources, the house deliberately used available standard components, such as windows and doors, and whatever bricks the builder could find. In the sense that it made use of whatever building materials happened to be available to the local builder at the time at a reasonable cost, it represented a twentieth-century enactment of the vernacular scenario. In practice the house ended up looking very much, from the outside at least, like any other speculative housebuilder's building. The lesson of the Sugden House was widely discussed in the architectural Press of the time.

In the USA more interesting examples were designed in 1965 by Charles Moore in Sonomo County, California. This condominium of weekend apartments constructed from rough vertical timber siding and set among the dunes of the Pacific shore looks rather like a group of fishermen's huts and lofts. And in *ad hoc*, if not vernacular fashion, when the money ran out for the interiors, an artist was called in to design a series of giant graphics over the rough, unfinished walls, creating the illusion of purposefulness.

With others, Moore was to develop the Sugden House-style vernacular idea, notably in the Talbot House, in California, whose basic form he worked out on the drawingboard but whose precise details he left the jobbing builder to work out for himself. Not entirely surprisingly, the house is full of incongruities and inconsistencies.

In a side development of this notion of the almost-all-rightness of the 'design' of untutored contemporary builders, architect Robert Venturi developed a set of theories which were based on the visual value of

Charles Moore's design for Sea Ranch Sonomo, California, 1965, in the manner of a collection of timber fisherman's huts and net-drying sheds (*David Gebhard*).

Charles Moore's Talbot House, Berkeley, California, 1967. Basic plan and layout provided by the architect with fine grain detail and construction method carried out by the builder (*David Gebhard*).

twentieth-century jobbing builders and sign-erectors – and on the virtues of modern architectural primitives, notably Simon Rodia, builder of the famous Watts Towers, and the Frenchman Ferdinand Cheval, whose bizarre Palais Idéal at Hautrive seemed to offer lessons for modern designers. In a sense, here were a group of modern architectural primitives stalking the Arcadian junkyards in search of whatever building materials could be found. Precisely what lessons could be learned was not quite clear – any more than what serious practical lessons were to be found in the eighteenth century from an observation of the primitive lifestyles of Noble Savages.

In fact, America already had designers of slightly similar ilk in Herb Green and Bruce Goff. Both these (trained) architects produced a string of fascinatingly bizarre houses which quite deliberately abandoned any interest in the traditional idea of what a house might look like. Organic, anthropomorphic, alliterative or whatever, they went beyond the boundary of what we could reasonably think of as being vernacular, although their choice of materials was of the same 'organic' palette.

These were all quite serious attempts at developing an unselfconscious twentieth-century vernacular approach to architecture which, unlike all the architecture of the past, was unencumbered by fashion, style and copybook decoration. This approach favoured earthy, woody materials put together in a deliberately casual fashion. The rather rambling shapes of this kind of

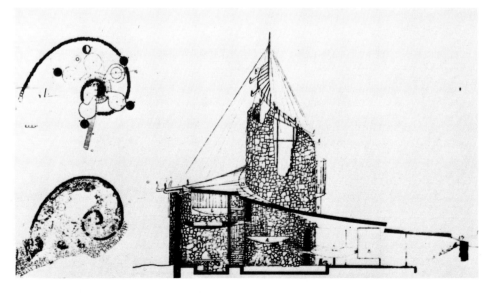

Design by Bruce Goff for a house for a lover of plants, 1951-7. This (built) design is based on a central stone core supporting a spiral roof and floors: natural form and natural materials for a nature-lover.

building hinted at the forms and *ad hoc*ness of real vernacular building without deliberately imitating them.

But with François Spoerry's late 1960s design for Port-Grimaud, imitation vernacular suddenly became almost respectable once again. Modern architects paid slightly horrified visits to this brand-new seaside resort at the base of the St-Tropez peninsula but came back not at all sure that it might not be almost all right.

One of the earliest of the seaside holiday apartment developments which have been a new phenomenon of European prosperity, Port-Grimaud is at first glance a genuine French fishing village, complete with cobbled square, conglomeration of old cottages, irregular pantile roofs, fading painted stucco, the occasional classical column or keystone half embedded in a wall, an old blockhouse at the village entrance, hanging flowers and an authentic air of having grown up over the centuries, only recently having been invaded by the motorboats and sloops of the newly affluent. In fact, it is all completely new. As a setting for a fortnight's escape from the world, it is precisely right – a three-dimensional stage set for the enactment of the simple life without any of the inconveniences of real primitive seaside peasant existence.

Not an old Mediterranean fishing village but the new town of Port-Grimaud on the St-Tropez peninsula designed by François Spoerry for summer visitors.

Port-Grimaud is twentieth-century Europe's answer to Blaise Hamlet. Its numerous imitations, which are now to be found right round the European coast to the Netherlands and the Scandinavian countries, indicate that the Anglo-Saxon dream has spread – and slightly changed its locus. In Europe it has become known dismissively as '*le style Club Mediterranné*' but it is one which developers have recognized as striking some kind of inner cultural chord, a slightly modified folk memory of Marie-Antoinette playing milkmaids beside the Hameau's little lake, the scale multiplied many times over in the transformation from the Versailles woods and water to the dunes and marinas of littoral Europe.

But Britain has the tradition of taking its fantasy seriously, and the cottage fantasy has now been invested with high social purpose by humourless housing designers and, for the most part, brought back into the countryside where it properly belongs. For those designers and their public housing committee clients, it is less fantasy than a solemn return to the alleged cultural and social traditions of the Anglo-Saxon past, an answer to the remorselessness of post-war modern housing design and an everyday way of housing people in the country – and, somewhat bizarrely, in the town as well.

Outside the holiday season the new European seaside peasant holiday villages are deserted, their transient occupants back in town getting on with everyday life. In Britain, because the occupants are public housing tenants, the fantasy surroundings are a permanent stage set in a way which is very little different from that of the dependent indigent occupants of Blaise Hamlet or Somerleyton or even Penshurst.

The two most sensational British Neo-vernacular developments are not far from each other in the east coast county of Essex – South Woodham Ferrers and Noak Bridge, both names which evoke a cosy, vernacular, almost Tolkienesque past.

The village centre of South Woodham Ferrers is an imitation Old English village set around an irregular village square. The centrepiece is an 'old' market hall with brick classical detailing – occupied in (real) traditional fashion by a bank, with solicitors upstairs. Around about, in a knowingly disorderly array, are imitation vernacular shops, a pub and a chain supermarket in the guise of a big Essex barn. It is a mixture of styles and periods in a patchwork of pastel-washed stucco, the occasional example of half timbering and brick nogging, irregular roofs, windows and doorways, jutting first floors and varied materials – tiles, slate, brick, pargeting (the local decorative plasterwork) and imitation stone. All are a little too sharp-edged to be properly convincing in the Port-Grimaud pattern, and the theatrical nature of the whole ensemble is revealed around the loading bays

South Woodham Ferrers – an odd, earnest imitation of an Old English village centre.

at the back and in the impossible-to-vernacularize car-park off to one side, although the filling station at its entrance boasts an accurately detailed Georgian roof, suspended in the air on steel stanchions. The housing surrounding this set-piece centre follows the same pattern but the sketchiness of 'vernacular' detailing and the orderly pattern of its street layouts reveal it for what it is – local authority and speculative private housing.

Not far away across the county at Noak Bridge the vernacular village illusion is more completely carried through. This collection of one-, two- and occasionally three-storey houses and flats takes the form of a vernacular village scattered tightly among a set of winding roads and backyard footpaths. It is a *tour de force* of cheap Picturesque inventiveness. There are little rows of nineteenth-century working-men's cottages with doors straight onto the footpath, a pub with a wall-mounted sundial, which turns out to be a block of flats, and a rather Victorian institutional building which is also flats. There are little octagonal tollhouses here and there straight out of late eighteenth-century pre-Picturesque patternbooks, irregular roofs, dormers, clapboarding, tiles, brick, and rendering (over concrete blockwork) in the slightly garish Essex vernacular pinks and blues, and blacks.

Here is a carefully disordered *mélange* of vernacular house types, of materials, details and shapes whose only give-away is the illiterate way in

Cottages at Noak
Bridge.

which some of the more idiosyncratic designs (such as the tollhouses) are
located – and repeated too often. The difficulty with designing reasonably
large estates in the Neo-vernacular style is the problem of avoiding too much
repetition.

South Woodham Ferrers and Noak Bridge are probably the most
successful imitation vernacular schemes in Britain, although there are many
others: imitation Yorkshire miners' villages and coastal Essex vernacular in
rural Buckinghamshire, imitation almshouses in village Hampshire, rural
row housing in metropolitan London, re-created fishing village vernacular in
seaside Cornwall (in give-away concrete blockwork with steep Picturesque
entrance stairs which are rather inconvenient for mothers with prams),
Victorian Builder's Gothic in Littlehampton, imitation Victorian terrace
housing in central London, and vaguely to middlingly vernacular in
practically every location where public or private housing is being
constructed.

Housing at Milton Keynes by Martin Richardson in the style of a Yorkshire mining village with front doors right on the village footpath.

Perhaps the most concentrated collection of Neo-vernacular housing is to be found at Milton Keynes, the British new town which began in a blaze of ultra-modern housing and factory design but which, in the face of severe criticism from conservative architectural critics, began to commission housing estates in a variety of Neo-vernacular styles, the earliest of which was a kind of neo-Victorian builder's vernacular.

The latest stylistic phase at Milton Keynes turns out, in a nice example of history repeating itself, to be in the Italian vernacular mode. Most of these houses are groups of four apartments put together to give the impression of a small villa – which Charles Parker and P.F. Robinson would surely have recognized as latterday variations of their favourite vernacular mode. And one or two individual cottages suggest that the Milton Keynes planners had access to designs published by J.M. Gandy in 1805, so close is the resemblance.

These latterday examples of the Italian vernacular style are also reckoned to be examples of Post-Modern classicism in the sense that they contain some familiar elements from Italian traditional architecture put together in a mannered, mannerist, eclectic way without too much concern for the niceties of historical accuracy. And it may be that this is to be the new branchline which the Picturesque cottage is to take this time round.

Italian vernacular flats at Milton Keynes (*Tony Weller, Builder Group*).

House for the painter Graham Ovenden by Martin Johnson designed in an almost fairytale style using local materials with decorations and details garnered from a dozen architectural sources.

Elsewhere in Britian, outside the public housing ambit, there are one or two individual idiosyncratic buildings which loosely belong to the broad church of Picturesque cottagery, such as the Ovenden House in Somerset, which is a delicately organized patchwork of stone, glass and ornament, veering in its near-Wonderland way in the direction of the traditional eighteenth-century garden folly. There is the town hall for the London borough of Hillingdon, whose rambling forms recall a mixture of giant Picturesque cottage forms mixed together with details and shapes which recall in part at least the ruined fortifications of medieval Europe; and there is the gothicky lodge-style Picturesque/Post-Modern headquarters of the high technology firm at Stone, Oxfordshire.

Post-Modern office at Stone, designed by Eric Parry using vernacular materials, vaguely vernacular forms plus a series of references to architectural details of other times (*Eric Parry*.

Billed as introducing 'humanity' into modern housing, the Neo-vernacular style has gripped the British housebuilding fraternity's imagination, for, quite apart from the Picturesque visual pleasures of the latterday cottage ornée, there is, for public housing committees, much the same satisfaction in being able to relate the architectural style of public housing to the economic status of the future inhabitants: peasant-style housing for twentieth-century improvidents.

Rarely is that expressed consciously, for few of the new protagonists of Neo-vernacular realize that theirs is not a new approach at all. Like their landowner and cottage-architect counterparts nearly two centuries before, they are imbued with a belief that older, simpler, more natural virtues can be inculcated in the peasantry by creating for them domestic settings which symbolize those long-gone golden ages. The wheel has come full circle.

Bibliography

Bibliography

Documents and Drawings

Aberdeen Papers: B.M.
BURN, William, drawings: RIBA.
(Cadland) Drummond Papers 1777-1837: in private possession.
LEE, C.W., sketchbook: V & A.
LEICESTER, G.O., notebook: RIBA.
PAPWORTH, J.B., drawings: RIBA.
POCOCK, W.F., scrap book: B.M.
REPTON, George Stanley, notebook: RIBA.
REPTON, Humphry, Red Book, Attingham Park: at Attingham.
—, Red Book, Bracondale, A Villa of Philip Matineau: Norfolk.
—, Red Book, Holkham: at Holkham.
REPTON, John Adey, notebook and drawings: RIBA.
WIGHTWICK, George, drawings: RIBA.
WYATTVILLE, Jeffrey, book of drawings: B.M.

Printed Sources: Nineteenth Century and Earlier

ADAM, Robert and James, *The Works in Architecture of R. & J. Adam*, London, 1773-9.
'AEDITUS', *Metrical Remarks on Modern Castles and Cottages, and Architecture in General*, London, 1813.
AIKIN, Lucy, *Memoirs of John Aikin M.D.*, London, 1823.
ALBERTI, (Leoni. trans.) *Ten Books on Architecture*, London 1755 ed.
ALISON, Archibald, *Essays on the Nature and Principles of Taste*, London, 1790.
BEHN, Mrs Aphra, *Oroonoko: or the Royal Slave*, London, 1688, reprinted in Henderson, P. (ed.), *Shorter Novels: Seventeenth Century*, Everyman ed.
BRANNON, George, *Vectis Scenery*, London, 1821.
BREES, S.C. *The Portfolio of Rural Architecture*, London, 1841.
BRITTON, John, *The History and Description, with Graphic Illustrations, of Cassiobury Park, Hertfordshire*, London, 1837.

BROOKS, Samuel H., *Designs for Cottage and Villa Architecture*, London, 1839.

BURKE, Edmund, *A Philosophical Enquiry into the Origins of our Ideas of the Sublime and Beautiful*, 2nd ed., London, 1787.

BURNETT (ed.), *The Discourses of Sir Joshua Reynolds*, London, 1842.

CASTELL, Robert, *The Villas of the Ancients Illustrated*, London, 1728.

CASTELLAN, A.L., *Letters on Italy*, London, 1820.

COCKBURN, James, *Swiss Scenery from Drawings by Major Cockburn*, London, 1820.

COZENS, Alexander, *A New Method of Assisting the Invention in Drawing Original Compositions of Landscape*, London, 1785.

EARLOM, Richard, *Liber Veritas or 200 Prints after Claude*, London, 1787.

EDGEWORTH, Richard Lovell and Maria, *Memoirs of Richard Lovell Edgeworth Esq.*, London, 1820.

EDGEWORTH, Maria, *The Absentee*, London, 1812.

EDWARDS, J., *A Companion from London to Brighthelmston in Sussex*, London, 1801.

FELIBIEN, *Les Plans et les Descriptions de Deux des plus belles Maisons Campagne de Pline le Consul*, Paris, 1699.

GILPIN, William, *Three Essays: on Picturesque Beauty; on Picturesque Travel; and on Sketching Landscape*, 3rd ed., London, 1808.

—, *Observations on the River Wye*, London, 1762.

—, *Observations; relative chiefly to Picturesque Beauty, ... the Mountains and Lakes of Cumberland and Westmorland*, London, 1786.

—, *Observations; relative chiefly to Picturesque Beauty, ... the High-Lands of Scotland*, London, 1789.

—, *Remarks on Forest Scenery*, London, 1791.

—, *Observations on the Western Parts of England*, London, 1798.

GIRARDIN, R.L., (Daniel Malthus trans.) *An Essay on Landscape*, London, 1783.

HOWORTH, Mrs. (ed.), *The Poems of Baron Haller*, London, 1794.

JONES, Edward, *Athenian or Grecian Villas*, London, 1835.

KAMES, Henry Home, Lord, *Elements of Criticism*, London, 2nd ed., 1839.

KENT, Nathaniel, *Hints to Gentlemen of Landed Property*, London, 1775.

KERR, Robert, *The Gentleman's House*, London, 1864.

KNIGHT, Richard Payne, *The Landscape, a Didactic Poem in Three Books*, 2nd ed., London, 1795.

—, *An Analytical Inquiry into the Principles of Taste*, 2nd ed., London, 1805.

KNIGHT, William (ed.), *Memorials of Coleorton*, Leicestershire, 1803-1834, London, 1887.

KRAFFT, J.Ch., *Plans of the Most Beautiful Picturesque Gardens in France, England and Germany*, Paris, 1809, 1810.

LABORDE, Alexandre, *Descriptions des Noveaus Jardins de la France*, Paris, 1808.

LAMB, E.B., *Studies of Ancient Domestic Architecture*, London, 1846.

LAUDER, Sir Thomas Dick, *Sir Uvedale Price on the Picturesque*, Edinburgh, 1842.

LAUGIER, *An Essay on Architecture* (English Edition), London, 1755.

LEEDS, W.H., *Studies and Examples of the Modern School of English Architecture*, London, 1839.

LOUDON, *A Treatise on Forming, Improving and Managing Country Residences*, London, 1806.

MALTHUS, Thomas, *An Essay on the Principle of Population*, London, 1798.

MARSHALL, *A Review of the Landscape*, London, 1795.

MASON, William, *The English Garden*, London, A new edition, 1783.

MATTHEWS (attr.), *A Sketch from the Landscape*, London, 1794.

MEASON, Gilbert Laing, *On the Landscape Architecture of the Great Painters of Italy*, London, 1828.

MORRIS, R., *Lectures on Architecture*, London, 1759.

PAIN, William, *The Builder's Pocket Treasure*, London, 1763.

PAPWORTH, J.B., *Hints on Ornamental Gardening*, London, 1823.

PAPWORTH, Wyatt, *J.B. Papworth, Architect to the King of Wurtemburg*, London, 1879.

PRICE, Uvedale, *Essays on the Picturesque*, London, 1810.

—, *An Essay on the Picturesque*, London, 1794.

—, See also LAUDER.

REPTON, Humphry, *Sketches and Hints on Landscape Gardening*, London, 1795.

—, *Observations on the Theory and Practice of Landscape Gardening*, London, 2nd ed., 1805.

—, *An Enquiry into the Changes of Taste in Landscape Gardening*, London, 1806.

—, *Fragments on the Theory and Practice of Landscape Gardening*, London, 1816.

—, (J.C. Loudon ed.) *The Landscape Gardening and Landscape Architecture of the Late Humphry Repton*, London, 1840.

ROSCOE, Thomas, *The Tourist in Switzerland and Italy*, London, 1830.

RUTTER, John, *An Illustrated History and Description of Fonthill Abbey*, London, 1823.

SHENSTONE, William, *Works*, London, 1764-9.

SMITH, J.T., *Remarks on Rural Scenery*, London, 1797.

STEVENS, Francis, *Views of Cottages and Farm Houses in England and Wales*, London, 1815.

WARE, Isaac, *A Complete Body of Architecture*, London, 1756.

WEIR, George, *Historical and Descriptive Sketches of the Town and Soke of Horncastle, in the County of Lincoln*, London, 1820.

WETTEN, Robert, *Designs for Villas in the Italian Style of Architecture*, London, 1830.

WHATELY, George, *Observations on Modern Gardening, and Laying Out Pleasure Grounds*, London, (new edition) 1801, (1st ed.) 1771.

WILLETT, Ralph, *A Description of the Library at Merly in the County of Dorset*, London, 1785.

WOOD, John, *A Series of Plans for Cottages or Habitations for the Labourer*, London, 1781.

WRIGHTE, William, *Grotesque Architecture, or Rural Amusement*, London, 1767.

ZIMMERMAN, Johann George, *Solitude Considered with Respect to its Influence upon the Mind and the Heart*, London, 1799.

Periodicals

LOUDON, *The Architectural Magazine*, 5 Vols., 1834-8.

European Magazine, 1803.

(ACKERMANN, Rudolph,) *The Repository of Arts Literature, Commerce, Manufactures, Fashion and Politics*, 1st. Series 1809-15; 2nd. Series 1816-22; 3rd. Series 1823-8; 4th. Series 1929 only.

Gentleman's Magazine, Vol. 72, 1802.

GROHMAN, Johann Gottfried, *Ideen-Magazin für Liebhaber von Gärten …*, Leipzig, 1797-1805.

GROHMAN, Johann George, *Ideen-Magazin für Architecten, Kunstler und Handwerkert, die mit der Baukunst und ihren Einzelheuten zu thun haben …*, Leipzig, 1835-45, 5 Vols.

The Builder.

The Mirror, 1830-33.

Monthly Review, 1795-1805.

Communications to the Board of Agriculture, Vols. I-ff., 1797.

(BAUMGÄRTNER, Freidrich Gotthelf,) *Neues Ideen-Magazin für Lieb-haber von Gärten, Englishen Anlagen und für Bezitzer von Landgüten ...,* Leipzig, 1806, 1 vol. only.

PAPWORTH, Wyatt, *The Architectural Publications Society Dictionary.*

Printed Sources: Twentieth Century

ALLEN, B. Sprague, *Tides in English Taste (1619-1800)*, New York, 1969 ed.

BARBIER, Carl Paul, *William Gilpin*, London, 1963.

BATE, Walter Jackson, *From Classic to Romantic. Premises of Taste in Eighteenth Century England*, Cambridge, Mass., 1946.

BOULTON, James T., *Edmund Burke*, London, 1958.

BURKE, W.J., *Rudolph Ackermann*, New York, 1935.

CARRITT, E.F. (ed.), *Philosophies of Beauty*, Oxford, 1931.

COLVIN, H., *Biographical Dictionary of English Architects 1660-1840*, London, 1954.

DARLEY, Gillian, *Villages of Vision*, London, 1975.

DAVIS, T., *John Nash the Prince Regent's Architect*, London, 1966.

FAIRCHILD, Hoxie Neale, *The Noble Savage*, New York, 1928.

GREEN, Candida Lycett, *English Cottages*, London, 1982.

HERRMANN, Wolfgang, *Laugier and Eighteenth Century French Theory*, London, 1962.

HIPPLE, W.J., *The Beautiful, The Sublime, and the Picturesque in Eighteenth Century British Aesthetic Theory*, Carbondale, 1957.

HUSSEY, Christopher, *The Picturesque*, London, 1927.

KAUFMANN, Emile, *Architecture in the Age of Reason*, Cambridge, Mass., 1955.

KAYE, Barrington, *The Architectural Profession in Great Britain*, London, 1960.

LESLIE, C.R., *Memoirs of the Life of John Constable Composed Chiefly of his Letters*, London, (Phaidon ed.) 1951.

LOVEJOY, A.O., *Essays in the History of Ideas*, Baltimore, 1948.

MANWARING, Elizabeth Wheeler, *Italian Landscape in Eighteenth Century England*, London, 1965 ed.

MONK, Samuel H., *The Sublime*, Michigan, 1960.

PORT, H.M., *Six Hundred New Churches, A Study of the Church Building Commission, 1818-1856*, London, 1961.

REDGRAVE, *A Dictionary of Artists of the English School*, 2nd ed., London, 1878.

ROSENBLUM, Robert, *Transformations in Late Eighteenth Century Art*, Princeton, 1967.

STROUD, Dorothy, *Humphry Repton*, London, 1962.

SUMMERSON, John, *John Nash, Architect to King George IV*, London, 1949.

—, *Heavenly Mansions*, London, 1949.

WATSON, J.R., *Picturesque Landscape and English Romantic Poetry*, London, 1970.

WHITLEY, W.T., *Art in England 1800-20*, London, 1928.

WHITNEY, Lois, *Primitivism and the Idea of Progress in English Popular Literature of the Eighteenth Century*, Baltimore, 1934.

WOODBRIDGE, Kenneth, *Landscape and Antiquity: Aspects of English Culture at Stourhead, 1718 to 1838*, Oxford, 1970.

WOODFORD, John, *The Truth about Cottages*, London, 1969.

Cottage Books

AIKIN, Edmund, *Designs for Villas and other Rural Buildings*, London, 1808.

ATKINSON, William, *Views of Picturesque Cottages with Plans*, London, 1805.

BARTELL, Edmund (Jun.), *Hints for Picturesque Improvements in Ornamented Cottages*, London, 1804.

BROOKS, Samuel H., *Designs for Cottage and Villa Architecture*, London, 1840.

BROWN, Richard, *Domestic Architecture*, London, 1842.

BURTON, Decimus, View of the rustic village now being formed at Furze Hill, London, Lefevre, *c.* 1838-41.

BUSBY, Charles Augustus, *A Series of Designs for Villas and Country Houses*, London, 1808.

CARLISLE, Nicholas, *Hints on Rural Residences*, London, 1825.

DEARN, Thomas Downes Wilmot, *Designs for Lodges and Entrances to Parks, Paddocks, and Pleasure-grounds*, London, 1823.

—, *Sketches in Architecture consisting of original designs for cottages and rural dwellings*, London, 1807.

—, *Sketches in Architecture, consisting of original designs for public and private buildings*, London, 1807.

DOMVILLE, Lady Helen, *Eighteen Designs for Glebe Houses and Rural Cottages*, London, *c.* 1840.

ELSAM, Richard, *An Essay on Rural Architecture*, London, 1803.

—, *Hints for Improving the Condition of the Peasantry in all Parts of the United Kingdom, by Promoting Comfort in their Habitations*, London, 1816.

GANDY, Joseph Michael, *Designs for Cottages, Cottage Farms and other Rural Buildings*, London, 1805.

—, *The Rural Architect*, London, 1805.

GOODWIN, Francis, *Domestic Architecture*, London, 1833.

—, *Domestic Architecture, Second Series*, London, 1834.

—, *Cottage Architecture: Being a Supplement to the First Series of Goodwin's Rural Architecture*, London, 1835.

—, *Cottage Architecture; Being a Supplement to the Second Series of Goodwin's Rural Architecture*, London, 1835.

GYFFORD, Edward, *Designs for Elegant Cottages and Small Villas*, London, 1806.

—, *Designs for Small Picturesque Cottages and Hunting Boxes*, London, 1807.

HALL, John, *Novel Designs for Cottages, Small Farms and Schools*, London, 1825.

HEDGELAND, J., *First Part of a Series of Designs for Private Dwellings*, London, 1821.

HUNT, Thomas Frederick, *Architettura Campestre*, London, 1827.

—, *Designs for Parsonage Houses, Alms Houses etc.*, London, 1827.

—, *Half a Dozen Hints on Picturesque Domestic Architecture*, London, 1825.

—, *Exemplars of Tudor Architecture, Adapted to Modern Habitations*, London, 1830.

—, *A series of designs for gate lodges, gamekeepers' cottages and other rural buildings*, London, 1826.

JACKSON, J.G., *Designs for Villas*, London, 1829.

LAING, David, *Hints for Dwellings*, London, 1800.

LOUDON, John Claudius, *An Encyclopaedia of Cottage, Farm, and Villa Architecture and Furniture*, London, 1842.

LUGAR, Robert, *Architectural Sketches for Cottages, Rural Dwellings, and Villas*, London, 1805.

—, *The Country Gentleman's Architect*, London, 1807.

—, *Plans and Views of Buildings*, London, 1811.

—, *Villa Architecture*, London, 1828.

MALTON, James, *A Collection of Designs for Rural Retreats*, London, 1802.

—, *An Essay on British Cottage Architecture*, London, 1798.

MIDDLETON, Charles, *The Architect and Builder's Miscellany*, London, 1799.

—, *Picturesque and Architectural Views for Cottages, Farm Houses and Country Villas*, London, 1793.

PAPWORTH, John Buonarotti, *Rural Residences*, London, 1818.

PARKER, Charles, *Villa Rustica*, London, 1832.

PLAW, John, *Ferme Ornée; or Rural Improvements*, London, 1795.

—, *Rural Architecture: Or Designs from the Simple Cottage to the Decorated Villa*, London, 1802.

—, *Sketches for Country Houses, Villas, and Rural Dwellings*, London, 1800.

POCOCK, William Fuller, *Architectural Designs for Rustic Cottages, Picturesque Dwellings, Villas, etc.*, London, 1807.

RANDALL, James, *A Collection of Architectural Designs for Mansions, Casinos, Villas, Lodges, and Cottages*, London, 1806.

RICAUTI, T.J., *Rustic Architecture*, London, 1840.

RICHARDSON, George, *New Designs in Architecture*, London, 1792.

ROBINSON, Peter Frederick, *Designs for cottages and Villas*. 1839.

—, *Designs for Lodges and Park Entrances*, London, 1833.

—, *Designs for Farm Buildings*, London, 1830.

—, *Designs for Ornamental Villas*, London, 1827.

—, *Domestic Architecture in the Tudor Style*, London, 1837.

—, *A New series for Designs for Ornamental cottages and Villas*, London, 1838.

—, *Rural Architecture*, London, 1826.

—, *Village Architecture*, London, 1830.

SOANE, Sir John, *Sketches in Architecture*, London, 1793.

THOMSON, James, *Retreats*, London, 1827.

TRENDALL, Edward William, *Original Designs for Cottages and Villas*, London, 1831.

Index

Index

———— • ————

References in *italics* indicate illustrations.